PRAISE FOR SUE TABASHNIK'S BOOKS

PATRICK SWAYZE The Dreamer

"It's a wonderful journey into the hopes, dreams, and sufferings of a great man. Throughout the book you show how Patrick fashioned his own life to conform with his spirituality and undying hope and resilience."

—*Joshua Sinclair, Director, Writer, Producer, Physician*

"Any Patrick Swayze fan will find this a wonderfully detailed account of not just his life events, but his personality, ideals, and the experiences of a woman who came to document his world."

—*D. Donovan, Senior Reviewer, Midwest Book Review*

"Tabashnik has gathered a wide range of interviews, statements and anecdotes to reveal a man who was talented, gentle, giving and who never gave up. Getting to know Swayze through the eyes of the author can help inspire anyone who wants to not only pursue their dreams but also see their dreams come true."

—*Dee Long, Editor*

"I highly recommend this book as it seems to connect to a deeper side of this amazing actor and dancer and it will refuel your passion for his work in film and as a performer—a great book to have!"

—*Patricia Mendoza*

"Thank you for giving his fans an in-depth look into a beautiful soul and his phenomenal legacy."

—*Lorrie Hardy*

The Fans' Love Story ENCORE: How the Movie DIRTY DANCING Captured the Hearts of Millions!

"A celebratory text packed with behind-the-scenes information on the producers, stars, and film team that includes an in-depth interview from producer Linda Gottlieb about its making, interviews and photos with story consultant and dancer Jackie Horner, and more."

—D. Donovan, Senior eBook Reviewer, MBR

"Just fabulous. Love you—love the book. I now will cherish it and all of our memories."

—Jackie Horner, Story Consultant, Dirty Dancing

"She did an absolutely wonderful tribute to the film and Patrick, as well as the cast."

—Holly Tuell

The Fans' Love Story: How the Movie DIRTY DANCING Captured the Hearts of Millions!

"Your book is both great journalism and original writing. It is a very positive testament to Patrick and his life as an Artist and the impact it had on others."

—Joshua Sinclair, Director, Writer, Producer, Physician

"The interviews with the people involved in the film are fantastic and give a rare glimpse into the world of Dirty Dancing and the Catskills."

—Jan Griffith

PATSY SWAYZE
Every Day, A Chance to Dance

Patsy Swayze

Every Day, A Chance to Dance

SUE TABASHNIK

PASSION
SPIRIT
DREAMS
PRESS

Walled Lake, Michigan

ISBN 978-0-9894086-6-0 (paperback)

ISBN 978-0-989-4086-7-7 (ebook)

PRINTED IN THE UNITED STATES OF AMERICA

FRONT COVER PHOTO CREDIT: Deborah Feingold/Corbis Premium Historical/Getty Images.
Patsy Swayze and Patrick Swayze, 1988.

Book and cover design: Patricia Bacall, www.bacallcreative.com

To my parents, Phyllis and David
To my brothers, Bruce and David
Always in my heart!

ACKNOWLEDGMENT
OF GRATITUDE

To Mr. Patrick Swayze,

Know that you continue to inspire and
make a difference in so many lives.

CONTENTS

Used with permission of Charlene Swayze.

Patsy Swayze.

INTRODUCTION

I have written this book to honor and celebrate Patsy Swayze. I hope that reading the stories of some of her students, colleagues, and friends as to how they were influenced by her will showcase what an icon and trailblazer she was and the extent of her influence on them and on the world. Many of her students continue to carry forward her legacy by following in her giant dance footsteps.

Patsy was an icon in the dance and performing arts world for decades as a dancer, teacher, mentor, and choreographer. Her work includes founding the Houston Jazz Ballet, teaching at the University of Houston, running her own dance studios, and choreographing for Theatre, Incorporated, Playhouse Theatre, and Hollywood movies. She inspired thousands of dance students, many of whom went on to become professionals in the performing arts, and instilled in all students a strong work ethic and set of values. With that said, she was most proud of her family and thought her greatest achievement was being the mother of five children.

Of course, Patsy had one very famous student, her beloved son Patrick, known as "Buddy" to family and friends. The book will touch on the relationship between Patsy and Buddy. Another renowned student is Jaclyn Smith, who kindly granted a full-length interview about her experiences with Patsy. In her role as choreographer for *Urban Cowboy*, Patsy taught dance steps to John Travolta, and that will be covered as well.

Patsy was a pioneer in opening her dance classes and her heart to all students, regardless of race, economic, or cultural background, and this was no small feat in the fifties and sixties in Houston. In addition, Patsy was known to be extremely philanthropic.

I want to thank the interviewees for their enthusiasm, support, and time they put forth for the book. Many of them said that Patsy's story needs to be told and she deserves recognition that she never fully received. I have attempted to place the interviews in the approximate time sequence of when the person first had contact with Patsy, so that her story can be told in a somewhat organized manner. Many of the interviewees had a lifelong relationship with Patsy.

Patsy Swayze continues to touch the lives of multitudes of people, including mine, for which I am grateful.

Credit: KMazur/Getty Images. Used with permission of Jaclyn Smith.

Jaclyn Smith and Patrick Swayze at the 12th Annual Elton John AIDS Foundation Oscar Party co-hosted by InStyle *in 2004.*

Used with permission of Charlene Swayze.

Jesse and Patsy Swayze.

BRIEF BIOGRAPHICAL AND FAMILY INFORMATION

Patsy Swayze was born on February 7, 1927 in Houston, Texas as Yvonne Helen Karnes. She was raised in Houston and nicknamed "Patsy." Her father, Victor Elliott Karnes, was a World War I pilot and geologist. Her mother, Gladys Mae Snell Karnes, was a nurse. She was the oldest of four children, with siblings: Kathryn "Kitty" Karnes Buildt (sister), Diana Latham (step-sister), and Elliott Karnes (step-brother).

Patsy married Jesse Wayne Swayze on August 6, 1944 while she was still in high school at age seventeen, just before he was shipped overseas to begin his stint in the Navy. Jesse became a mechanical engineer and was nicknamed "Big Buddy." He died suddenly at the age of fifty-seven from a heart attack in 1982. Patsy and Jesse raised five children: Vicky, Patrick, Don, Sean, and Bambi. Vicky died from a suicide on December 2, 1994 at the age of forty-five. Patrick (nicknamed "Little Buddy" and then "Buddy") died from pancreatic cancer on September 14, 2009 at the age of fifty-seven after battling the illness for almost two years. Bambi (born "Bora Song") died December 15, 2021 at the age of fifty-five.

After the success of choreographing *Urban Cowboy*, Patsy moved from Houston to Simi Valley, CA in 1981 with Jesse and three of their children.

Patsy suffered a stroke on September 8, 2013 and died from complications on September 16, 2013 at the age of eighty-six at her home in Simi Valley, CA.

Credit: Fitzroy Barrett/ZUMA Wire.

Patrick receiving his star on the Hollywood Walk of Fame on August 18, 1997 (his birthday), flanked by his mother, Patsy Swayze (left) and his wife, Lisa Niemi (right). Back row from left, Don Swayze and Sean Swayze, his brothers, and his sister, Bambi Swayze.

Credit: Lois Williams. Courtesy of Barry Dean.

From left to right: Jan Gillory, Vicky Swayze, Barry Dean, and Doug Threeton. The photo was taken by Barry Dean's mother, Lois Williams, in 1972, at Patsy's studio where she was helping the four students with their vocal show called "Patchwork." They were preparing for a half-time show at Houston's Astrodome.

Credit: Bill Logan.

Bob Ritmiller and Vicky Swayze in a 1971 play by Bill Logan.

Used with permission of Charlene Swayze.

The Swayze Men: Brothers (top, from left) Patrick, Don, and Sean horsing around with their father, Jesse Swayze (center).

Used with permission of Charlene Swayze.

Patsy and Jesse with students.

Credit: Charles Bush.

Jaclyn Smith.

CHAPTER ONE

JACLYN SMITH

Actress, Designer, Entrepreneur, Philanthropist, Mom, Grandmother

Interview: March 9, 2020

I really appreciate that you agreed to grant this interview for my book on Patsy Swayze.

I tell you, she was an amazing woman. You can ask me anything that you want about her.

Okay. Thank you.
I read that you started dancing at age three.

Yes.

At what point, did you become a student of Patsy Swayze?

I started really in classical ballet. I didn't become a student with Patsy until I was around twelve. So I started with a more Russian technique with a teacher called Florie Olenbush. She retired and Patsy took over Florie's studio.

It was a total departure from anything I had been taught because Patsy incorporated everything with a complete discipline of the dancer: from jazz to tap, even to—as they called it then, not gymnastics, but acrobatics—and classical ballet. I guess *musical comedy* was the high point of her teaching for me. There was a community theater called Theatre, Incorporated. She encouraged us to audition for it. That was all new to me, performing live on a stage. It opened up a whole other world to me. I really was more of a classical dancer.

She was just the kind of teacher that made you go out on that limb and go to the areas that you weren't secure in. She opened up a whole new world. And she gave you every reason to be the best you could be. She was just this kind of person that you couldn't try hard enough for, because when you're good, boy did she let you know—but I mean, you really had to be good, so a compliment meant the world. It wasn't, "Okay, let me just dial in a compliment." Not only did she compliment your strong points, but she gave you the criticism of what you needed to work on.

It sounds like the criticism was done in a constructive way.

Oh, absolutely, never to destroy your sense of self. We learn from our criticism. And as an actress, or dancer, or performer, in general—I mean, you welcome criticism because it's the only thing that's going to make you better. She had trained so many professional dancers. She would travel to New York and bring back interesting choreography, including choreography of Jerome Robbins. I remember we did *Bye Bye Birdie* and we had all the original choreography that she would incorporate and teach us, even if we weren't in that particular show.

She choreographed a lot of shows at the Theatre, Incorporated.

Did you know Patsy throughout her life?

Yeah. And I knew her children. Patrick—Buddy, as I knew him.

He and Lisa did some contracting at one of my houses here. He was really starting his career and I had already done *Charlie's Angels* and we reconnected. I saw him throughout.

I saw Patsy, but not as much because I was here and she was in Houston, but we'd touch base on the phone. And every now and then we'd get together with all the students, whether it would be—Pat Cope [Mackenzie], Patrick, Candy Tovar, and Margo Sappington, all those students that went on to do really interesting things.

I think the fascinating thing about Patsy is, you looked at her, and she was really beautiful, young, and she could do anything. She just had a charisma. So you couldn't help but look at her, you didn't want to take your eyes off her movement, her expression. She just was very charismatic, very charismatic. She had a way to inspire us to be the best we could be.

You know, when you move away, you always wish you had seen more of the person because then all of a sudden someone's gone, and you think, they were so important in the beginning of my career. You know, introducing me to musical comedy really made me think in a different way. I thought I was going to be a ballet teacher and open a school in Houston, but because she introduced me to the wide performance, the stage musical comedy, I ended up going to New York, still to study ballet, but [then] came home. But because of her training, I started auditioning for summer stock and one thing led to another, and then I did a pilot for a television series, and at one point that television series happened to be *Charlie's Angels*.

She was instrumental in paving the way for all of that, of giving me this linear direction to what a career should be and how you accomplish it.

When you were talking about Patsy, it seems like that's where Buddy got a lot of his stuff from. You said Patsy could do anything and she was charismatic. It's sort of where Buddy got all that from.

Yeah, and they both had this like very tawny, natural-quality tawny skin, natural hair. You know when I say sensual and sexy, there was a cleanness about it. She was still this girl next door, but yet she was so naturally free in her movement and her approach to people. You just wanted to sit down and talk to her. You liked her. She was approachable and she was unique. She wasn't the typical ballet teacher. She had this long hair parted on the side, sort of like women wore their hair in their forties. Sometimes it would be pulled up, sometimes just washed and dried naturally, very beautiful.

Of course, Patrick was like that, too. You couldn't have gotten a more beautiful dancer, very masculine, and yet, gosh, technically as good as anybody.

Do you have a theory as to why Buddy became the star out of the five kids?

Oh gosh, you know, it's about magic and he had it. He was the oldest. No, I really don't know. I think there was a lot of talent in that family, but I think he was the closest to Patsy in just stature and body language and shape. He might have wanted it more, too. It's not always *why*. It's how hard you try and how hard you go after it. She was a disciplinarian with her children and she really pushed them in many directions. Some take that as a springboard to go forward and some stop.

How many people make it to the height that he made it? Very few, very few.

If you could speak to Patsy now, what would you say to her?

I would say thank you for making me go out on that limb because that's where the fruit is. Thank you for pushing me. Thank you for making me understand the discipline of what a career is, in that: It isn't just performing, it's the homework you do and the everyday carry-through. That's what I'd say. She gave me a sense of discipline about dance. When I think about it, yes, I had a natural turnout, a good extension, good elevation—but it takes so much more than that to do that day-to-day.

I think being a dancer is one of the more difficult art forms. You have to constantly be on top of it and I think she instilled that in us. But she also instilled in us to find ourselves on the stage, to not be a robot, to bring joy to it, to bring whatever our emotional feeling was at that time. She tapped the emotion to what we were doing.

Do you still dance?

I dance with my granddaughters. I do Pilates. I wish I had kept it up in a more consistent way because I think you need it for your brain, you need it for your body. So I do work out. I don't necessarily go to a dance class, but boy, I'd be better for it, if I had continued with some of that training. I'm very body-aware. I'm very much into keeping flexibility and muscle tone.

That's wonderful. What would you say Patsy's legacy is?

It's her students who have carried on her spirit and the love of her. Patrick is the perfect example. I think anybody that she's taught would honor her. That would be a wonderful legacy. She enlightened and inspired so many young people.

FINAL COMMENT: She's a great lady, and she should have a book.

WHAT PATSY SAID ABOUT JACLYN

From the Official Jaclyn Smith Website. Used with permission of Jaclyn Smith.

"She was one of those extraordinary young people who always seemed to have a sense of purpose and focus. I always knew that whatever she chose to do, she would do it, and do it well."

"Her fame and her exposure in the media has never changed her as a person. She's still sweet and herself and kind and friendly, and that's wonderful, I think. She has never let the industry make her different."

Credit: Jim Jongebloed. Used with permission of Renee Broussard Jongebloed.

Renee Jongebloed and Patsy at Jones Hall.

Credit: Jim Jongebloed. Used with permission of Renee Broussard Jongebloed.

Renee and her children Jimmy Jr. and Jenee with Patrick.

CHAPTER TWO

RENEE BROUSSARD JONGEBLOED

Dancer, Teacher, Choreographer

Interview: September 8, 2020

Thank you for sending the photos.

I also have other pictures. My daughter Jenee [Jongebloed Bobbora] is looking through one of her scrapbooks to see if she can find a couple that I know were taken of Patsy and her. We were with Patsy in New York at the World Jazz Dance Congress a couple of times. Oh, she reminded me that in New York, our camera was stolen.

Oh, my goodness.

Tell me, if you don't mind—I am curious to know how you become interested in Patsy. I gather you are a fan [of Patrick]. The great "love" of my life.

Yes. I first noticed Patrick—Buddy in *Dirty Dancing*. Of course, right?

Yeah.

Then I saw him on the Barbara Walters interview, the first one she did in 1988. I just thought, wow, this guy is not only so talented and handsome; he's a really great person. He's very interesting and very human. He didn't seem like the typical celebrity. So I started following his career. I joined the Official Patrick Swayze International Fan Club. People from all over the

world were in it. I made some friends.

Buddy came to Detroit for two fundraisers here [2002 and 2004]. He came with Complexions Contemporary Ballet, a company out of New York. He was on the board of directors. And so of course, as I was about a half-hour drive away from the Music Hall, I wasn't going to miss it. He introduced the company. The company danced. Many of the dancers were in his movie *One Last Dance.* He hosted a reception at the Detroit Athletic Club (a private social and athletic club) to raise money for Complexions. The company is cool because they do outreach with inner city kids, including here in Detroit. So those were the two times I met him in Detroit.

A lot of members of the Official Patrick Swayze International Fan Club showed up in Houston for the premiere of *One Last Dance.*

Note from author: *Patsy was one of the four choreographers of the movie.*

I was there.

It was just sort of mind-boggling.

Yeah.

Way back, I think in 2003.

It was 2003. I can tell you a really neat story. It makes me cry.

Oh.

My daughter Jenee, who is now fifty years old—thank you, Jesus—was diagnosed with inflammatory breast cancer in 2003. Inflammatory breast cancer is really bad. I don't know if you know much about it, but you should. It's rare, but it's automatically in your lymph nodes when you discover it.

Bottom line is Patsy was certainly by my side through so many things, even long distance. We knew the movie was coming. She called me a couple of times to be there. Great, we will be there—Jenee and I, probably even Jimmy, my son who is three-and-a-half years older. Jenee was diagnosed. I had told Patsy I think the day that we got the diagnosis.

The day of the opening of the movie was when she started her first day of chemotherapy. It's the type of chemo where you come home with the bag and the machine and the whole thing. She had a two-year-old little girl. So she was coming to my house, staying with me while her husband took care of the daughter so she wouldn't have to see her mom with the chemo. We got home and got her in the bed. My husband was still alive at the time. He was a wonderful, wonderful man. She said, "Don't forget about the opening tonight. Mom, you've got to go." "I'm not leaving you." "Oh, yes, you are. Patsy would be so upset if you're not there."

My son picked me up. We went to the theater. Were you there?

Yes.

The tickets are all sold out. Jimmy and I are standing over by the doors. I was a nervous wreck anyway with leaving Jenee at home. She was thirty-two at the time she was diagnosed. We're standing there. We'll see Patsy when she walks in and we'll tell her what's going on and then we'll leave. All of the lights and all the wonderful stuff with Buddy and Lisa walking down the red carpet, behind them was Patsy, of course. I let Buddy get by me, as fifty million people were taking pictures.

Patsy stepped up and gave me a big hug, and said, "Where's Jenee?" "Patsy, she started her chemo today and she's not going to be here and there are no tickets left. I just want to give you a hug." She grabbed Buddy from behind the neck, pulled him around, and said, "There are no tickets left and Renee and Jimmy are here." He put his arm around me, and he said, "You stay right by me. You're not going anywhere." Just so damned sweet. So we sat with Patsy, and Patrick, and Lisa watching the movie.

Wow! What a great story! That's what he was like.

He was just a doll, you know. He'd come in town, I'd see him about every five years. It wasn't like I'd see him very often.

Another time, he was here with his Arabian horses. We were out at the Ten Oaks Table. Patsy had written me. I knew a lot of people with the Houston rodeo. She said, "Let's see who all we can get who might be interested in some of these horses." And so I sent out some calls and stuff. Jim and I and my two children had just come in from snow skiing. We were exhausted, but I knew that the function was going on. And of course, Jenee for sure didn't want to miss it 'cause she knew that Patrick would be there.

We get there and Patsy is sitting downstairs eating barbecue. We sat with her. Buddy was upstairs with the crowd and the news people, being interviewed. It was a long, deep hall. We were getting ready to leave, and I said, "You give him a kiss from me 'cause he's going to be too busy." Patsy said, "You're not leaving here 'til you go see him. You all go upstairs right now." So we went upstairs.

This is really a very special story I have said many times to my children. We went into this long hall and he is at the other end being interviewed by some television reporter with a microphone. I said, "Oh Jim, oh gosh, I'm not going to say anything. I'm too embarrassed. I don't want to bother him with all these people here." And he looks over, down the hall, and he waves, and I looked behind me to see who he is waving at. Then he has that fabulous walk. He said, "Renee?" I said, "Buddy, I can't believe you even recognize me. I haven't seen you in so long." He said, "I will never forget the most beautiful smile in the universe." Of course, my Jim was standing right there, and he said, "I agree with you."

He was just that kind of guy, you know. He was always going to make you feel better about yourself, which of course was the way Patsy was too. She was a constantly uplifting person, and I want to say a "pusher," because she pushed you to do your best. Buddy got it from her and he got it from his dad. His dad was the same way. Big Buddy was just a dear, loving [guy], always a smile, always a compliment. They just were both so precious together.

Yes. Do you want me to tell you more about how I got involved in this?

Yes.

I was at the Houston premiere as well. I would say there were about thirty people from the fan club who flew in from all over the states and also some came from Europe. The president of the fan club, Margaret, made many of the arrangements for the fans' time in Houston. It was just the most amazing experience.

It really was and such an amazing show, the movie. I watch it a lot. I have it on DVD.

Buddy took time out to talk with us folks from the fan club, and so did Patsy. That was the first time I met Patsy. Patrick, Buddy—I don't know which name to use—he took group photos with us. They had us sitting right behind the family and friends to watch the movie.

The next day after the premiere, we were on a tour bus. It might sound a little hokey, but we were going to see some of the sights: the place where Patrick and Lisa got married, one of the first family homes, and so forth.

So who gets on the bus? Patsy! She said, "Patrick is going to get on the bus and you can ask him any questions that you want, and he asks kindly, please don't take any more photos because his eyes are still sensitive from last night." We were all like, well of course, we are not going to take any more photos. So the two of them talked to us for almost an hour. We could ask anything we wanted. It was cool.

Note from author: *It was really enjoyable to watch the fun-filled and respectful banter between Patsy and Buddy.*

The night before, I had talked to Patsy on a one-to-one, just very brief, a couple of minutes. You know, it was mobbed, like a thousand people at the reception. Buddy's running around with no security, at least at first. I talked to Patsy and she was just so impressive.

When I returned home, the author in me wanted to find out more about Patsy, but at that point, there really wasn't that much information on the internet about her. So I kind of let it go. Later on, I thought she seemed like such an amazing person; so I got the idea for this book.

Patsy was everything. There wasn't much that Patsy didn't do. I'm sure you know she taught swimming. She taught ice skating. She taught roller skating. She was just such an athlete and so determined to do well.

I tried to make a phone call to the woman who owned the dance studio in Houston on Memorial Drive, in a very lovely part of Houston, where I was teaching part-time. I never wanted to have my own studio because I didn't want to be leaving home when my kids were coming home [from school]. I had my degree in elementary education, but I decided I didn't want to do that. I was able to teach [dance] part-time. Patsy was having problems at the particular studio she was in. You know, Patsy was big on letting students take classes for free. That was really an important thing to her.

That's what everyone says.

She knew I was teaching in this really nice, big studio. She said, "I need to get into another studio." She asked if I could help her, so I connected her to the woman who owned the other studio, Billie Pucciarello.

Billie was just about the opposite. You had to pay your money upfront. They were like oil and water. It wasn't that long that Patsy was there, but it served a purpose for her. It was fun for me because I got to be around Patsy and watch Buddy walk in and out. So that was a very neat, involved dance thing that I had with Patsy as an adult.

My daughter Jenee, I would drive her out to Ella Boulevard to the Southwest Jazz Company along with several of her friends.

When did you first meet Patsy?

That's a neat story, too. It was kind of by chance. I didn't know anything about Patsy. I was probably thirteen (in 1957). I had taken lessons for years from a dance studio in Houston that was the popular dance studio of Virgie Lee Emmons. I love her to death because she made me love dancing, but she was not a technical ballet teacher. I had gone to a recital of a neighbor friend of mine when I was like twelve. She was with a real, classical, Russian-trained teacher, Florie [Olenbush]. So I switched from Virgie to Florie.

Jaclyn Smith said she had taken classes from Florie.

She was with me. That's where we knew each other. Ellen was a year younger.

You said Ellen, not Jaclyn?

Ellen was her name [what she went by].

From the author: *Jaclyn Smith was born Jacquelyn Ellen Smith per IMDB. Ellen was raised in Houston.*

She went to Lamar High School and she was one of my friends at Florie's studio. Florie had a baby and decided to stop teaching. I don't know how they connected, but Patsy bought her studio and that was the studio on Richmond. That's how I met Patsy, by chance. I was going to stick with that studio and I was blown away because I had gone from kind of a fun, little dance teacher who taught you how to sing and do tap and acrobatics to a classical ballet teacher—and now here's Patsy doing jazz. That was really fun. She made sure that you had the ballet training behind it.

She really was the new wave, the new thought that was behind dance in Houston. She was very involved with Theatre, Incorporated doing choreography. Then she was the director.

I'm kind of skipping around. You know how many movies she choreographed. Do you have *Liar's Moon* listed? She did the choreography. It was a teenage show and she needed a teenage high school student to be in a scene that happened at the school gym. My son was a football player at the time. It was like in 1982, so that would have been his freshman year in high school. She called me and said, "Get Jimmy and tell him to get some friends. I need you all to come to my house so I can teach them how to jitterbug for the movie." So we did. We got four of his friends. We had the best time going to her house. . . .

So that was shortly after *Urban Cowboy* [1980].

I was in that movie [*Urban Cowboy*]. Only because of her! Patsy called me. "Do you want to come out to the set and help me direct people and move people around?"And so I did, along with a girlfriend of mine, Beverly, that she adored. Beverly wasn't a dancer, but Patsy knew her. Beverly had a ranch and was interested in some of Buddy's horses. So that was a really fun experience, to be out there on the set with her. I am in a scene [doing] club dancing. We're up on a balcony. John Travolta and the other love interest are dancing below us. I'm in *Urban Cowboy* for maybe two seconds, but it was such a fun experience being with her on set. And Buddy was there [watching]. . . .

There are things that came out about Patsy being mean, all that trash. It just drives me crazy. You can turn anything you want to into that, but she was a driven person for herself. I never saw her being mean. I've seen her be stern and pushy as far as making someone repeat something and practice and try to better oneself. I would never attribute that characteristic to her.

That's what people are telling me, that she was not mean.

Another thing about Patsy was she realized what Jenee was going through and she called me at least every two weeks just to check on her. I mean for her to be as busy as she was and to keep that in mind was just unreal.

Yeah, that's the type of person she was.

She was and she loved my momma. My momma was an unbelievable seamstress and she made all these beautiful clothes for Patsy.

Patsy would introduce me when I would walk into the studio in college, when I had stopped taking class on a regular basis. I was in a sorority and all of that stuff in college. She would stop the class and introduce me as Miss University of Houston. I had some notoriety with different things at the University of Houston that were in the paper, but she would always make it so much bigger.

That's sweet.

Yeah. It made you feel good. Like Big Buddy did. They were just that kind of people.

Of course, the horrible loss of Vicky, that was so hard on her.

That was so sad.

They were heartbroken.

Yes.

Is there anything else that you want to say about your dance career?

Mine was mostly in the form of teaching and choreography.

I was raised, and Patsy understood, in a very strong Catholic family and went to an all-girl high school here in Houston, St. Agnes. When it came time to do shows at Theatre, Incorporated, Mom just wasn't going to let me do it. I didn't particularly want to. I might have to wear a really risqué costume (not by today's standards, but back then) and I would not be very well-accepted at St. Agnes Academy. It was never a big desire.

I loved teaching, that's probably why I wound up getting a degree in teaching. I chose, instead of teaching school, to teach dance for most of my adult life.

When did you stop teaching?

I stopped when my daughter graduated from high school. I got busy building a house, and had so much stuff going on with my husband. We traveled a lot. I had a wonderful husband that she adored and he adored her. My husband's name is Jim. He passed away four years ago from lung cancer.

I am sorry.

So my teaching was just real part-time, off and on. In high school, I taught at a studio before I even knew Patsy. I taught at a studio when I was a freshman for a lady that was here in Houston, taught full-time there. I taught the ballet troupe at my high school, which was kind of funny because the ballet troupe was given PE credit, and I was a junior and senior teaching these kids who were getting credit.

Do you still dance?

I had one knee replacement and I need to get the other one done. It makes me so sad because I taught ladies' ballet exercise class before it was ever real popular and real glamorous to do at the studio for Billie. Billie Pucciarello is where I taught most of my studio [classes].

Of course, for my daughter's high school, I did the tap and jazz choreography for their shows. The other thing I did kind of professionally was my women's organization here. It's national, actually. We used to put on a charity show called The Houston Junior Forum Showtime at Jones Hall here. We would hire a director from New York who would come in for three weeks and teach the different shows. It was all members who participated in it. I did the dance choreography for that; it was always fun for me. I've always kind of had my finger in it. Patsy always got a kick out of me participating in it.

I'm going to be seventy-six pretty soon, in January. I do miss it a lot.

I have my granddaughter who is a dancer. I even have a little dance studio in my house. I try to do as much as my body will let me.

I understand.

But it's always in my heart.

If you could talk to Patsy now, what would you say to her?

I love you. And I would thank her. She was always there when I needed her, when my mom died and then when Jenee was diagnosed.

What I hate more than anything is that, after Buddy died, I maybe had one phone call with her, and then she just didn't accept any calls after that. It was real hard. I would talk to Donny or maybe somebody who would answer the phone.

Why do you think, out of all of the kids, Patrick became the star?

That is a good question. I think it's more about Patrick than it is about Patsy. The physical attributes of this guy. He was a great football player. I think it is more about Patrick's desires. I don't think that

Patsy said, okay, I'm going to make him into a fabulous ice skater—you know, he skated in the Ice Capades—and then a dancer. I think he watched his mom and that's what he wanted to be and do. He took hell for that in Texas, being a dancer and also in a Texas high school playing football. He got a lot of bullying.

Oh.

You know, it was just the way it was back then. Texas was all about football. If he hadn't had such a horrible injury to his knee, he might have wound up being a professional football player.

Wow. He was so talented.

Yes, so talented. Patsy was really big on keeping that masculinity in style. I know one of the dancers that he looked up to so much was Gene Kelly. He always reminded me of that style when I watched him. I still think Patrick was the most masculine, classically-trained ballet dancer I've ever seen. Even with his technical abilities in classical ballet, it was so masculine, and a lot of male ballet dancers don't have that.

Lisa was so wonderful [in *One Last Dance*]. When I watched that movie, I'm pretty positive that Patsy was sitting next to me, and she was so quiet during that movie. It was just like tears constantly in her eyes. All I remember her saying is, "You know, he was fifty years old when he filmed that movie." I think she was amazed that he could do all that at that age.

Yes, that's true, that was amazing. They trained for like three or four years really hard before they started filming. I guess he was having trouble with his knee.

One of the movies that Patrick made, *City of Joy*, was fabulous. I got a postcard from Patsy that said, "Get all your friends to go see this movie this weekend because the theaters are not going to carry it." There was something going on in the world. That movie failed, but it's a great movie. He is just wonderful in it. It had a great message, too. I thought, how cute, for Patsy Swayze to be sending me a postcard to go see her son in a movie, but that's how she promoted. She didn't care, you know: "Do whatever it takes."

How about when he played the drag queen in *To Wong Foo [Thanks for Everything! Julie Newmar]*?

I don't know what her thoughts were on that. She probably didn't love it.

I do know that she told him that *Dirty Dancing* was a bunch of fluff, and said, "Don't do it." You've heard that, I'm sure.

Yes.

I can see her right now when we were in New York together at the Dance Congress, and she said, "Can you believe this? Can you believe I said that?"

Well, the main people involved, the cast and crew, really took it to another level. It could have been just fluff.

The choreographer did and obviously the dancers.

And then it was just meant to be for Patrick. I can't believe they're going to like drop another one, as that would be just a disaster.

That's crazy. Jennifer Grey is one of the producers and stars.

Well, we'll see. I don't know who will be doing the dancing. Nobody is going to compare to him.

FINAL COMMENTS: It is sad to think about Patsy. She was a very special person in my life. When you have to name five people who influenced you in such a good way, she is pretty much at the top of the list.

Used with permission of Renee Broussard Jongebloed.

Patsy, Renee, Jenee, and Bambi at a dance workshop in Houston.

Used with permission of Barbara Geary, Robert Levitt, and Patricia Cope Mackenzie.

Patricia Cope Mackenzie with Ethel Merman (in her dressing room) for the Broadway production of Hello, Dolly *in 1967.*

Used with permission of Patricia Cope Mackenzie.

Patricia Cope Mackenzie in The Roar of the Greasepaint-The Smell of the Crowd *Broadway production in 1965.*

CHAPTER THREE

PATRICIA COPE MACKENZIE

Theatre, Inc. Alumna, Professional Dancer, Broadway Performer, Choreographer

Interview: June 23, 2020

When did you first meet Patsy and under what circumstances?

I had been taking dancing when I was about thirteen years old. I guess most people would say, "Ooh, that's an old lady." I was taking strict ballet from a Russian teacher and she got pregnant and decided to sell the studio and Patsy was taking over. I had never done anything more than just ballet, toe, and character dancing. Well, Patsy came in like a whirlwind, and taught not only ballet, but jazz and musical comedy, and tap, and more character, and gymnastics, and I mean, just everything. And she was definitely a powerhouse.

What do you mean by "a powerhouse?"

She was nonstop. She couldn't stop talking. She was talking about her kids who had gone to New York and California and how beautiful all these students were and how wonderful that you were coming to my classes, even though you lost your teacher. And the whole class I think went over to her. So many of her regular students were just dynamic because they'd all been with her for a long time. They'd been in shows. And I thought, "Oh, my gosh, I don't want to be a ballerina anymore. I want to be in show business."

It was the beginning of a wonderful, fun, inventive, and educational experience with Patsy. She was just amazing. Everybody looked up to her. She just took everybody under her wing—some talented, some not so talented—and made us all feel incredible and that we were the only thing in her eyes. Of course, at that age, you're willing to have people tell you what you shouldn't be, as long you're told you are beautiful and talented and everything. She was never tearing anybody down. She just built everybody up and made us all feel like we were going to make it in the world.

That's sweet.

I was thirteen or fourteen maybe. So I'm seventy-seven now. That was probably in the fifties.

How long did you know Patsy?

Well, until she died. She was in Houston for a long time and I lived in Houston for a long time. Then I went to New York with her blessing and met a lot of people that she knew and met a lot of her old students and did a lot of stuff. Then I got married and we moved out here (California) in '75 and Patsy moved out because Patrick was here. We called him Little Buddy. His dad's name was Big Buddy. They all moved here.

When Little Buddy was little, we were all in ballet class and doing all kinds of stuff. He was dancing around with us, but he was a little thing. . . . Who knew he was going to develop into such a wonderful man?

How old do you think he was at that point?

Probably around eight, nine, ten.

He was just starting out, not really dancing, but sort of being in the classes and trying to play around with the steps and things. Then I guess she officially put him in the classes a little later, when she felt he could handle it. Then he went on from there.

She came out here and then she started doing movies and various things. You know, we were still in touch. We'd go out to her studio in Simi Valley, just play around and stuff.

Then I got sort of out of the business. My husband was a television director, so I started choreographing a little bit for him. Then when we had our kids, I really became a parent. I was at the school and doing all kinds of stuff, ultimately becoming their school librarian. So that was my second career.

Patsy was just a wonderful inspiration because I saw how she handled her students and the shows and how she choreographed. I pretty much patterned a lot of my things on her. I didn't think about it then, but I think a lot of things I did in choreographing sort of came by osmosis through her. I was doing things with my husband on television. She did a lot of stuff. It was wonderful because she was always saying, "Don't dance it, don't make it *dancey*, make it real." So I always kept that in the back of my mind. I think I was more successful doing that because we had some friends who are choreographers and they worked for my husband, and he said, "There's too much dance, it's too *dancey*. Try to make it more real. Keep it simple." Gene Kelly, our champion, always said, "Keep it simple. Simple makes it better."

If you could talk to Patsy now, what would you say to her?

Thank you so much for putting me on the map. I appreciate what I got from you and what you've taught me, not just in the world of dance, but in the world—getting along with people and how to work with people. That really follows through in everything. I mean in business, and raising children, and keeping a marriage. I've been married for fifty-four years. The things she said, she didn't throw them into our heads, she just gave it to us. Things like that always stick, I think.

Thank you [to] Patsy for being the wonderful person that she was.

Do you think she realized how much influence she had on so many people?

I think ultimately she must have, because so many people were just so grateful to have her in their lives. You know, she pushed. She didn't settle for second-best, but it made it worth it. I think you never know how much you touch people, until you're gone, actually. You really don't know. She touched a lot of people.

I didn't realize when I started this project how big it was going to turn out. I am grateful to all of the people participating in the book.

How did you come to be doing this?

As you can imagine, I was a super-big fan of Patrick, or Little Buddy. This all started sort of by accident back in the *Dirty Dancing* days. I then shared the story that I had told Renee Broussard Jongebloed in the last chapter about the two Complexions events in Detroit and the meeting-up in Houston for the *One Last Dance* premiere in 2003, during which I met Patsy.

What about contact with family members of Patsy? We already talked about Buddy a little bit. Did you want to say anything else about Buddy or anyone else?

My husband and I did several shows at Theatre Under The Stars in Houston. Vicky was her oldest daughter. We hired her and so we got to catch up with her life, and her children, and her talents, and everything, and so that was fun.

We were with the kids as we were growing up in Houston together.

Did you go to school with any of them?

No. They lived out in more of a rural area. We were in more of a suburban area.

Jaclyn [Smith] and I went to two different schools that were semi-rivals. But everybody hung out together because the drama departments were so close.

Donny was just a tiny thing, not like now. Sean came much later, after I had left town. I had gone to New York by then. So I really didn't get to know him. Then it was sad when Vicky died.

What a tragedy.

That was so sad.

She was fun to work with. Growing up, I hadn't really known her all that well, but it was fun [working] with Vicky. Little Buddy was the only one who came around the studio and just hung out. [Patsy's] grandchildren, we never really knew. I went to New York in '64. That was all of the contact I had with the kids.

What about Big Buddy?

Oh, Big Buddy, so sweet. He was such a teddy bear. Everybody loved Big Buddy. Oh, my gosh, he was just so incredible. Then they came out here and we were so excited to have them all out here. And then, bam, he went and died. It was very difficult on all of them. He was really the *mensch*. He was the guy. He was so supportive of Patsy and the family. You know, he was always there. He was the rock. As far as I was concerned, I would have loved to have had him as my daddy.

All of the things Patsy was involved in, it seems like she couldn't have done all of that without Big Buddy.

Oh yeah, exactly. He was really supportive. He hung out with them. She was even teaching swimming lessons.

I heard that.

She was constantly on the move. She just was one of those who had tons of metabolism. She smoked a lot, like a chimney. She was thin and just so active. Not only did she teach swimming there, but she also took on handicapped children and those who had been in accidents to rehabilitate. She took handicapped kids and taught them ballet: it was to strengthen their legs, to strengthen their bodies. And she helped people who had been in accidents, to rehab them and strengthen their bodies. I mean, when did she do all of this?

The story goes, she was in an accident and her mother put her in dance to rehab.

Right, and I think that stuck with her. "Okay, I'm going to do what they did for me and pay it forward."

That's cool.

It was so amazing. People that they said were never going to walk again, and they were walking.

No one has told me this part. I'm really glad you are mentioning it.

It was not something she tooted her horn about. It was one of those philanthropic things that she just felt the need to do. It was very admirable, I think.

One other question about Little Buddy. Do you have any idea why, out of all of the kids, he became the star?

You know, some people have that *it* factor. Some people are extremely talented and they can work so hard, but they can get just so far, because they don't have that *it*. He had the spark, that thing in his eye. There was a toughness, but a vulnerability to him, and that's what you need to get through to people and to make people sit up and take notice. That was one of the things that he had in spades.

That makes sense.

He wasn't just handsome. He didn't play up his handsome. He almost played against it. He was a football player and he's dancing. He's a ballet dancer and a football player. So he was everything. People loved him on the team and people loved him on the stage. He just was that. People are just born with it. You can't teach it.

Every time we saw him I would call him Little Buddy. It is very hard for me to call him Patrick.

Right. Is there anything else you want to say about Patsy?

She was just always encouraging us to go beyond ourselves. "If you want to dance, great, but you have to sing, too, then you have to act. You can't do just one thing. You have to be a well-rounded person." We all strove to do that.

She was a Big Band singer before she started teaching, I guess. When she was young, she traveled with big bands and she would sing. I remember her big song was "I Cover the Waterfront." She was always breaking into that song. It was really funny. By herself, she would be listening to music or doing something and sort of singing it low, in her head. *What are you singing Patsy?*

She was all things to all people. She was a mother, a teacher, an educator, a compadre, a compassionate therapist, a babysitter. She was everything. Everybody wanted to be with her.

I heard of people living at her house.

Yeah. She had such a big heart. I owe a lot to her.

Say a little bit more about New York and California, and being a choreographer. How many years were you a choreographer?

I wasn't a serious choreographer. It was just sort of on the outskirts. I was a Broadway dancer. My first Broadway show was *The Roar of the Greasepaint -The Smell of the Crowd*. It was with Anthony Newley and Cyril Ritchard. And then I did several others. A thing called *How Now, Dow Jones*, and believe it or not, the theme was the Dow is going to hit one thousand.

Do you stay in touch with any of the other people who were connected to Patsy?

We did for a long time, and then we moved out here and lost touch a bit. I caught up with Jaclyn a few years ago. We go in and out of touch.

The one thing that I wanted to say about my career is that I performed in *Hello, Dolly* with Ethel Merman, you know, at the end of the run as Ermengarde (the character is her niece and she's always trying to get her married off). My husband did Cornelius in *Hello, Dolly* with Ginger Rogers, Betty Grable, Martha Raye, and Carol Channing. We never got to do it together. . . .

When do you think that was?

That was '68, '69. We got married in '66 when my husband was working with Ginger Rogers.

That's cool.

We did two tours together as a couple. So that was kind of fun. We did the *Apple Tree* and he was the lead and I was the dance lead. Then we did *Promises, Promises*, and he was the lead and I was the dance lead and dance captain in both. That was really great. He started directing and he directed me in a lot of stuff in summer stock.

When I left home, it was really hard to say goodbye to Patsy, but she would say, "Fly. Go fly. You've got to do it." Very encouraging, always very encouraging.

Actually, Jaclyn and I were in *West Side Story* together at our local theater in Houston. She came from a wonderful family. We did a lot of shows together in Houston at our local theater.

She has posts on her website about Patsy. It's really nice.

Oh, she does? I'll have to check it out. How lovely.

FINAL COMMENTS: I'm glad you're doing this to promote her memory.

I think there is a story here to be told.

Everybody knows the man [Buddy], so this is the woman behind him. If it weren't for her, he wouldn't be here.

People miss him.

He left us way too soon. We all miss him.

Used with permission of Blake McIver Ewing.

Blake McIver Ewing.

Used with permission of Susie Ewing.

Susie Ewing.

CHAPTER FOUR

SUSIE EWING

Former Original Dean Martin Golddigger, Dancer, Singer, Actress, Teacher

BLAKE MCIVER EWING

Singer, Dancer, Actor, Choreographer
Son of Susie and Bill Ewing

Interview: July 14, 2020

When did you first meet Patsy and under what circumstances?

Susie: I grew up in Houston. I lived there from the time I was little. I was born in Denver, but we moved when I was a baby to Houston because my parents were from Texas originally.

At five years old, my mother took me to see *An American in Paris*. When I saw that movie, I said that's what I wanted to do. So she enrolled me in the local dance school. By the time I was about nine years old, my teacher there—thank God for her—said, "Susie has learned all she can from me. You need a better teacher. Take her to . . ." Patsy was on that list of teachers, but at that time we lived on opposite sides of town. Houston is real spread out, so it was very hard to get there. So we went with the one that was closest to us, which was Maxine Asbury. I started with her probably at eight years old, maybe nine years old.

By the time I was eleven, Maxine Asbury created the Houston Civic Ballet Company for Houston (which is now their professional company), but at that time, she was the ground floor. She was starting it. She brought on her board all of the top teachers in Houston and Patsy was one of them. So that's how I first met her. Every Saturday I went to the ballet company from nine o'clock in the morning until five in the afternoon. I just clasped on to all these fabulous teachers, and Patsy was one of them. I did end up going to her studio, and that's where I met Patrick. I'm about six years older than Patrick. He was a little boy when I was a teenager. He was always running around the studio and dancing.

I moved to Los Angeles and I got my career started. Actually, I was at the Houston Music Theater when my career started. The director hired me and brought me out here for *The Dean Martin Show* and *The Golddiggers Show* because they needed a Golddigger. I didn't know Francie [Mendenhall] yet. Francie ended up being a Golddigger as well, because she got hired out of Houston. We became good friends and realized we knew a lot of the same people.

Note from author: *Per Wikipedia, "The Golddiggers was a female singing and dancing troupe that performed in the style of Las Vegas showgirls. The group was formed in 1968, dissolved in 1992, and reorganized in 2007, and has numbered between four and thirteen members over various time periods."*

How long were you in the Golddiggers?

Susie: Five years.

Wow.

Susie: I did all of the Dean Martin shows at the time, and we also had our own series, *Dean Martin Presents The Golddiggers* (that was his summer replacement show). So I did all of those.

I did the tours in Viet Nam. Three of those: 1968, '69, and '70. That was unbelievable. That was the best thing I ever did in my career, outside of getting to dance with Gene Kelly.

You danced with Gene Kelly?

Susie: Yes, in Vegas and in a television special. Our Golddigger producer also produced other musical shows. He put together a show called *50 Girls—Count 'em, 50*. It was a big musical variety show and Gene was the star of it. We did a television special first and I got to dance in that. But then we took the show to Vegas and we had a contract at the International Hotel in Vegas, which at that time was the largest stage in the city. It was a magnificent show.

I bet.

Susie: That was the next biggest thing I did.

I have heard Patrick being compared to Gene Kelly by some people.

Susie: Well, I think because of his athleticism. Patrick was a very strong male dancer. That's what Gene was like. I had never heard that before, but I can see it. It makes sense.

Did you stay in touch with Patsy?

Susie: Well, here's what happened. You know, I went on to do my career. She knew that I was a Golddigger and all that. When Blake was five years old [1990], he just was singing and dancing around the house constantly. My husband and I both knew that he had a voice, nearly perfect pitch at five years old. So I started looking for places to take him. My girlfriend Rosie, who had been a Golddigger with me, had a little dance studio. I took him there, actually when he was three. Wasn't it Blake?

Blake: Yeah.

Susie: He was very disciplined, even at three. He won't tell you all this, but I will. So I took him there. I would have taught him anything he needed. I was a dance teacher, too, but I didn't want it to come totally from me. I thought it was better to have a teacher that was not mommy. He did very well there. Loved it, had a blast. And then I ran into another friend of mine, who said, "Did you know that Patsy lives in California now? She's right out in Simi Valley. She's fifteen minutes from you. She would love to teach Blake." I went, "Oh, my gosh!" So I drove out there and walked in the studio and surprised her. She didn't recognize me. I said, "Patsy, here's who I am. Do you remember?" "Oh, my God." So we had a whole reunion. And then I told her about Blake, and that I thought he really had potential. She said, "Bring that kid to me!" Of course, she fell in love with him the minute he walked in the door. He never missed class. He worked so hard.

Blake, how old were you at that point?

Blake: I was about four. I was in her little baby ballet class. I started tap at her studio. What really was a turning point for me was a group of performing kids that worked out of the Swayze dance studio on the weekends called Onstage Kids. The guy who started it was Bill Edwards, and Patsy and Bill were very close. So he used the studio on the weekends during the mornings when there weren't dance classes going on. I started in that group, and that's what got me singing. That really changed my trajectory, even though I continued to dance throughout my life, on and off. That was where I really honed the beginning of what became a singing career for me.

Patsy is the reason that I got my first television gig. I was trying to work my way up to one of her younger competition dance groups. I was still too young to be in the group that I was trying to be in, with the older kids that I was looking up to. I had been doing so much with this weekend group, Onstage Kids, and Patsy knew that I was singing a bunch. So she invited me to sing a medley and tap dance, but do a medley of patriotic songs. This was near the Fourth of July at this dance competition. She was going to let me perform while the judges tabulated. I was too young to compete. So I did perform, and one of the judges at that dance competition was Tony Charmoli, who was the director of *Star Search* at the time.

Susie: Everybody gave him a standing ovation.

Wow.

Susie: Needless to say, the judges weren't judging 'cause they were watching him when they were supposed to be judging. When Blake took his bow and left the stage, Tony stood up, and said, "Who are the parents of this child?" Bill and I raised our hands. He came to us, and said, "Blake is going to be on *Star Search*. I found the next winner, but he's got to come and formally audition." Patsy was there.

Blake did win for the entire year of 1992. He was the junior vocalist champion.

That's amazing.

Susie: Patsy was there and Mr. Bill was there. They were all there for the final.

What happened next with your career, Blake?

Blake: After winning *Star Search*, it was kind of amazing. Now we're so saturated with so many competition shows, but in the early nineties, *Star Search* was the only one. So a lot of people who won kind of worked out of the *Star Search* office as an unofficial agent for, you know, the launch pad of their careers. A lot of people did it. I was no exception to that. I got a bunch of auditions just from industry people calling the *Star Search* offices and asking about me.

One of those calls was the producers of the TV show *Full House*. They had written an episode that was loosely based on a performance that I did on *Star Search*, which was also sort of another version of the original medley in Patsy's competition that got me the gig on *Star Search* to begin with. It was this patriotic medley that ended with "Yankee Doodle Dandy." A couple of the *Full House* writers had seen me do it on *Star Search* and thought, "Oh, wouldn't it be funny if we write this talent show and Michelle thinks she's going to get the part and some kid comes in and takes it out from under her?" They wrote this idea based on my performance, but they didn't know if I could act, or, you know, put three words together.

So I came in essentially to audition for a role that was sort of written for me, but not guaranteed that I would do. Then I went in and sang the number and then did the reading audition, and within a day, I was at the table read with the whole cast. That was sort of crazy, 'cause literally I had watched them all on TV. I was a fan of the show as a kid, never thinking that I would have the opportunity to be on it. I ended up spending two more seasons. I was a recurring regular for two and then a contract regular for the final of the show.

That's amazing. So were you guys in touch with Patsy later on?

Blake: Yes. I kept up, you know, sort of in and out. I wasn't as consistent 'cause I was busy doing other things. About a year, or maybe not even a full year after *Full House* wrapped, I was cast in an NBC TV movie of the week. They were doing the third *Problem Child* film. They were going to do straight to television. I cast as one of the villains in it and part of the character arc was that he tap-danced.

Susie: You were a tap star.

Blake: Yeah. I was playing a vicious, horrible child star. So we contacted Patsy because they didn't hire a choreographer. They had no clue. They were so out of their depth. They hired a director and producer who had never done any musical content whatsoever. They didn't hire a songwriter to write the song for the talent show thing at the end. And then they hired me to do all of this stuff. So we brought in Patsy. *We know somebody who can choreograph this.*

That's great.

Blake: And she did.

What do you guys remember most about Patsy?

Susie: It was her dedication and the fact that she was tough, but she was not mean. She knew if you had potential, she had to knuckle down and pull it out of you 'cause you were a kid. She responded to kids who loved what they were doing.

It was just her dedication to her family. I think she was toughest on her family.

I've heard that from other people.

Susie: Yes. I think she was, but it was literally all out of love. She never demanded more from you than she demanded from herself. She was tough on herself. And I think that's the kind of performer she was.

No one has said that before, so I am glad to hear that particular thought.

Blake: The thing about Patsy was that no matter how old you were, she demanded your best. It was like you said, it was in a way that was not intimidating, which was really fascinating because you read about or hear about the style of dance teachers. I think it's sort of a derivative of the Russian ballet technique, where you know, it's like the woman in the corner with the cane banging it on the floor. . .

Susie: Or on your leg.

Blake: Yeah, and everyone is in fear. Patsy never drove from a place of fear. It was always from a place of excellence. So she was demanding, definitely, and she was difficult, definitely—but it was in this crazy, supportive way. I specifically remember never being intimidated or afraid in her class. When I started taking dance in other places, I was like, oh, this is that scary moment where you're afraid in class. I never had that with her, even though she was super tough.

The other thing that was so fascinating about Patsy is she had this wicked sense of humor.

Susie: Oh, she did.

Blake: She was hysterical. She was enough: really funny, and really sarcastic, and really dry. At a time when I didn't really know what those things were, I just knew that I liked her because of it.

She would wear those clips in her hair on either side of her head and she'd push that hair back into the clip as she was barking some order across the floor. It was hysterical. "Be careful. Now do that 8 count again!" usually with a cigarette in her mouth.

She was just one of a kind. There was nobody like her.

Certainly, it seems that way, you know.

Blake and Susie: Yeah.

If you could talk to her now, what would you say to her?

Blake: Thank you. I owe a lot to her. My career would not have taken the path that it took if it had not been for her because, literally, she unlocked the first important . . . Without her, I never would have gotten to Tony, and that changed everything. Without any drama attached to it, I really do legitimately have her to thank for my career.

Susie: I would thank her. I had lots of wonderful teachers, but like Blake said, she was just special. What I learned from her as a dancer and also as a person, I would thank her, too. It stayed with me through my life.

Susie, you mentioned Patrick earlier. Did you have much contact with Patrick or any of the other family members?

Susie: I knew Donny and I knew Bambi, not real well, but enough, you know, to say hello when I saw them in the studio. Blake, do you want to tell the Patrick story?

Blake: I talk about this a lot on my own show because the very first recital I did in Patsy's studio—the first award, the first trophy I ever got—was given to me by Patrick. So talk about setting yourself up for unrealistic expectations in show business! Literally, I'm a little four-year-old kid, and the first trophy I ever received for dance is presented by Patrick Swayze. Kind of ridiculous!

Susie: And that was after *Dirty Dancing* and all that.

Blake: Oh yeah, a huge movie star. Yeah. That was like '89. So he was like at the height of his world fame.

Susie: [Patsy would] bring Patrick in for the recitals, you know, meet the kids, and give out the awards. It was fabulous.

That sounds amazing.

Susie: It was. Of course, towards the end of his life, we didn't see him. I went to Patsy's funeral. I was there. Blake didn't get to go. I think you were on the road.

Blake: Yeah.

Susie: I was so glad that I was able to go. It meant a lot to me. My friends that are dancers were there. We lost a great lady.

It's just amazing, what she accomplished and how she accomplished it. So many people she taught.

Susie: Yes.

What else about Patsy do either one of you want to say?

Susie: We loved her and she was a huge influence on both of our lives. If you had told me when I was a dancer performing, *"Oh, your son is going to work with her,"* I wouldn't have believed it. It's just the way it happened was very magical, and we were just blessed by her. So glad that happened. Like Blake said, I truly believe she was the catapult of his career.

In summary, Susie, how long were you taking dance from Patsy?

Susie: Probably from the time I was about eight or nine through the ballet company, actually until I left Houston, which was eighteen. On and off, let's say nine to eighteen years old.

That's quite a while.

Susie: But it was on and off, like I say.

Do you have any theory about why Patrick became the star out of Patsy's kids?

Susie: It may have been that he sort of was the male Patsy. Wasn't he?

Blake: Very much so. Yeah. He definitely had his mom's sensibility for sure. I recently re-watched *To Wong Foo (Thanks for Everything! Julie Newmar)* and Patrick is literally doing Patsy. He's not playing a drag queen. He's just playing his mother. I hadn't even remembered it because I was so young when I saw it the first time. Having re-watched it, it was shocking and wonderful: just like a tongue-in-cheek tribute to her, without ever being mentioned.

Note from author: *Patrick told Bryant Gumbel in a 1995 interview for* TODAY *that Patsy was one of the women he modeled his character Ms. Vida Boheme on, along with Demi Moore, Lauren Bacall, and Audrey Hepburn.*

I don't think she was happy about him being in the movie. At least, that's what the rumor was.

Susie and Blake: Probably not.

I think he got nominated for a Golden Globe for it.

Blake: Yeah, I mean it's a great movie. I think he really captured her in it.

Also, I think Patrick just had that sort of *it* factor. You know, that bone structure that he inherited from his parents, like that onscreen (before we were messing with our faces as much and filtering everything)—just his bones, forty-feet-high on a screen, were captivating.

Susie: They were.

Well, he was pretty hard-working too, right?

Blake: Very much.

Susie: Very hard-working. But there again, that was Patsy saying, "Okay, you're a dancer." So she demanded the best of him.

Of course, Lisa [Patrick Swayze's future wife], that's how they met. She was taking classes back then. To my knowledge, they didn't know each other before then.

Susie, are you still dancing?

Susie: Yes, I am still dancing. Up until the COVID, I was teaching two classes a week, adult tap. I performed, I guess, it's been a couple of years since I've done performing. I still love it. You know, I have my aches and pains, but I still dance.

That's wonderful.
Blake, what's going on in your career?

Blake: A bunch of different things. I stayed in various parts of the business throughout my whole career and kind of jumped around all over from producing to directing to choreographing, acting a little bit less now, but doing a bit more behind-the-scenes things. I've actually done quite a bit of in the past year, actually quite a bit of choreographing, which would never have happened without Patsy.

That's really wonderful.

Blake: I'm not the greatest dancer in the world, but I found that I'm a better choreographer than I am a dancer.

Susie: He's being way too modest. He is a great dancer, but he's also a really creative choreographer. He's done some great things.

Used with permission of Susie Ewing.

Susie Ewing and Dean Martin from The Dean Martin Show.

Credit: Bill Ewing. Used with permission of
Blake McIver Ewing and Susie Ewing.

Patsy, Blake McIver Ewing, and Bill Edwards.

Credit: Bill Ewing. Used with permission of Blake McIver Ewing
and Susie Ewing.

*Blake McIver Ewing receives his first trophy at age 4 at
Patsy's studio given to him by Patrick Swayze in 1989.*

Credit: Blair Pittman. Used with permission of Pamela Mistrot Rost
and Valena Westmoreland.

*In the front is Pamela Mistrot Rost and in the back is
Valena Westmoreland, members of the
Houston Jazz Ballet Company, 1969.*

CHAPTER FIVE

PAMELA MISTROT ROST

Actor, Singer, Dancer, Teacher, Choreographer, Charter Member of the Patsy Swayze Houston Jazz Ballet Company

Note: This is a combination email and telephone interview.
EMAIL INTERVIEW: March 3-5, 2019

When did you meet Patsy and under what circumstances?

In August 1959, I was about to enter the third grade. My mother asked me if I would like to take dancing lessons. I replied, "Yes!" We went to a nearby studio. It was small and right next to my elementary school on Richmond Avenue and Timmons Lane in southwest Houston. On the day that we went to register for class, KILT radio station stopped by the studio. There was much excitement as they were passing out "KOOKIE" hats. They gave me one and I was instantly mesmerized by this exciting and electrifying environment. The office was run by hip-looking high school seniors. A beautiful girl with long, strawberry blonde hair sat at the front desk while a boy named Rick [Palmer] buzzed around like a bee. All of this was super exciting for an eight year old, as I had teenage siblings that kept things hopping at our house.

We waited for the class to be over so that we could meet the owner, Patsy Swayze. The door opened and a slender, young woman dressed in a blue tunic embellished with pink rick rack greeted us. She had long, wavy brown hair. Her crystal blue-green eyes sparkled like her smile as she showed us around the studio. I remember her asking, "So, would you like to take one or two lessons a week?" We decided on two lessons: ballet and jazz.

How long did you know Patsy?

I began taking dancing with Patsy at age 8 in 1959 and we stayed in touch until she died.

What did you learn from Patsy? How did she influence you?

My life was not disciplined when I met Patsy. From the beginning, I realized that ballet training from her was going to create something new in me, something that was missing in my home life. She instilled in me that ballet is the foundation of all dance, in that ballet steps and terminology have been categorized and can be translated to any form of dance in the world. In other words, I can observe a dance from an African tribe and name the steps as they loosely pertain to ballet. Patsy insisted she was a ballet teacher first, although she was acclaimed for her American jazz choreographic style and technique. She ranked in the top ten jazz dance teachers in the world, my stats. She was well-versed in all forms of dance, especially tap. Patsy Swayze was an amazing tap dancer.

To this day, I am very prejudiced against dancers who say that they've never studied ballet seriously. Patsy was a meticulous technician. She would painstakingly break down a simple step until it was perfect.

She believed that there are no "stars." She practiced her belief that every child has gifts and talents and that she was there to bring those out. I was one of those children who she struggled so hard with. I had no rhythm and was very uncoordinated, but Patsy never stopped praising me and encouraging me. I became a dancer and teacher and choreographer because of her persistence.

Patsy was pure Irish Catholic and had graduated high school from Incarnate Word Academy of Houston. She studied with nuns. She mentioned God to us frequently and "The Lord's Prayer" dance number was one of her most profound concepts in a choreographic work. She allowed others to actually choreograph the piece, but the concept was hers. It was always our most well-received dance number and always requested. Patsy was deeply religious.

For all of our lives, the main point Patsy drove home to us was "never quit." She had zero respect for quitters. Don't get me wrong, Patsy adored each of her children, but she demanded super-human results from them. She cut them no slack. Patsy did not tolerate excuses from her students or her own children. If you missed a class because you were ill, Patsy let you know you were not eating right, not taking your vitamins. Patsy and Big Buddy were both athletes and respected the human body and followed strict ideals regarding maintaining health, though sadly, Patsy was a chain smoker.

A favorite saying of hers—and she had many—was "Can't never could do anything." So we would avoid using the word "can't" at all costs, or we would surely hear the saying right afterwards. We were so loyal to Patsy that what she told us would override what our own mothers said. My mother would get so mad at Patsy (there was never any confrontation that I am aware of) because I would ignore what my mother said and follow Patsy's instructions.

At age thirteen, Patsy recruited me as her personal demonstrator. I rode the bus from school, dressed full out in pink tights, ballets, black leotard and hair secured in a classical bun. We started class with the little ones at 3:30 p.m. and I demonstrated for every class until the last class at 7:30 p.m., which was my class. I would get home at almost 9 p.m., eat dinner, and do homework. Many nights I just fell asleep in my leotard and tights. I demonstrated for all of her classes, Monday through Friday, throughout high school. This is how I paid for my classes. Patsy was so generous! Probably one third of her students didn't pay for classes at all. Her generosity is legendary, though not great business-wise.

Patsy was the hardest working human being—next to my father—that I have ever seen. People have remarked throughout my life about me that, "You are so determined. You never give up!" Patsy instilled this in us. "We try 'til we die." And anyone you meet who trained with Patsy will exhibit the same trait.

She was amazing. I loved her so much!

What do you remember most about your contact with Patsy's family?

As far as the other Swayzes, Big Buddy was so handsome and a very intelligent breadwinner as an engineer. We saw him most days at the studio. When I was a little girl, the TV show *Davy Crockett* was a popular weekly series starring Fess Parker. I used to think Big Buddy looked exactly like Fess Parker, so I had a crush on him.

Donny looked on from a playpen when I first began classes. Patsy had another studio in Oak Forest at that time. Vicky and Patrick were at that studio, so I rarely saw them until I was eleven, and Patsy teamed up with George Ballas, the inventor of the Weed Eater [lawn-trimming device]. George invited Patsy to bring her studio to the Almeda Road Fred Astaire Dance Studio. That is where Vicky and I became friends. It was at this time that Patsy became pregnant with Sean. Talk about "a little tow-headed terror"! Hahaha! Sean lived to disrupt Patrick's life, just to get his big brother's attention.

Patsy continued with George Ballas' invitation to move with him to his new, 42,000-square-feet Dance City USA on Richmond Avenue. This is where Patsy chartered her dance company, Patsy Swayze's Houston Jazz Ballet Company. We began performing for oil tycoon George Mitchell at various high-dollar charity events held at The Shamrock Hilton. After we performed, we sat at the table with many Hollywood starlets. To a thirteen year old, this was stardom.

At one of our first rehearsals at The Shamrock, in the fancy Emerald Ballroom, tables were in our way. Patsy flagged down a man whom she thought was a custodian to assist her in moving the furniture out of our way. The man was dressed in work chinos, but he was none other than the chairman of the event, George Mitchell. Patsy and George laughed about that for years to come as we became good friends with George and his wife. George even had a pool party for Patsy's company dancers at his mansion. George grilled hamburgers for us and took us on a tour of his new mansion being built on Memorial Drive, complete with a bomb shelter. What fun and amazing days these were. Patsy kept us busy dancing all over town.

In 1966, Jesse Jones Hall opened. It was Houston's newest luxurious music hall. Patsy's company was the first dance company to perform on that brand new stage. Also, please note that Patsy was totally oblivious to racial discrimination. One of her finest students was a drummer she picked up from the University of Houston. His name was Bill Chaison. Bill started out playing drums for our jazz class and Patsy started training him to dance. Keep in mind that 1966 was the height of racial tension in the South. Patsy didn't give a hoot about that. She paired college man—African American Bill Chaison—with a fifteen-year-old white girl, *me*, in a *Pas de Deux* on the debut of dance in the brand new Jesse Jones Hall. She was something: light-years before her time! Always bucking social norms in favor of what her Catholic upbringing said was the right thing to do. Got to love her! She was giving dance lessons to special needs children long before it became popular in the public eye. There never has been, nor will [there ever] be another Patsy Swayze.

Note from author: *Pamela shared that in addition to being a dance partner to Bill Chaison, she also partnered with Buddy Swayze and Ray Schmitt.*

Then there was Bambi. We were located in the little former country club on Judiway when Patsy announced that she and Big Buddy had adopted a little girl from Korea. All of the dancers in Patsy's company were there when Big Buddy and Patsy introduced us to their little, beautiful, four-year-old baby girl.

What do you remember most about Patsy?

Patsy never forgot anyone. It was a remarkable talent. If you had taken one class from her, she considered you her student. She truly loved everyone!

Of course, I remember her saying "Pamela." Her voice was unique, a bit raspy, probably from smoking, and she had a tiny little kind of whistle or lisp (barely noticeable), but it made her speech very distinctive. She was careful to enunciate her words perfectly and used lovely voice inflection. Whenever I see a picture of her in my mind, I hear her voice.

She wore glasses, and the poor glasses were oftentimes the vehicle of her displeasure when her company dancers were playing around and not being serious about rehearsal. She would either snatch her glasses off and toss them on the desk or snatch a record off of the turntable and Frisbee it across the desk. When this happened, we knew that she was seriously put out with us, and usually rehearsal on our dance numbers was stopped midstream and she started giving us a very difficult technique class to snap us to attention. Yes, she could get exasperated with all of us and her own kids especially.

Anyway, my memory of Patsy is like a second mother. We spent probably more waking time with Patsy than with our own dear mothers. We all wanted to please her. We all wanted to make her proud.

What did Patsy say about how she was trained to dance and why she became a dancer?

Patsy was raised in The Heights. Her dancing, I believe (not positive), began as rehabilitation from an automobile accident. Her teacher was Marcella Donovan Perry. Marcella's studio was located on 19th Street in the heart of downtown The Heights. I have been in the building in search of where my teacher studied dance. Marcella became the president of Heights State Bank. I never met Marcella, but I did meet Patsy's mother one time: a very energetic, wiry, Irish lady with a huge, contagious smile. Patsy spoke of Marcella, but not often, not in the way Patsy's students speak of her. However, seeing that Marcella went from dancing teacher to woman president of the bank, it's very evident that Marcella's impact and drive to accomplish must have had on Patsy.

Patsy did go back and forth to New York, at least one or more times a year, to study dance with her pal "Luigi."

Note from author: *"Luigi" was the nickname for Eugene Louis "Luigi" Faccuito who was a jazz dance legend. He once said, "To dance, put your hand on your heart and listen to the sound of your soul."*

From my earliest recollection, New York City was drilled into my brain as the only place on Earth to set my sights. Patsy made us all Broadway-bound, and some actually made it there and live there to this day. Candy Tovar and Bill Logan are two of Patsy's students who were on-and-off Broadway performers who still reside in New York.

Candy was my idol. I broke Bill's nose in class while doing a grand battement. We laugh about it every year and on birthdays and send snide Facebook posts to commemorate the bloody event that ensued on Bill's nose. Bill is a successful theatrical director in NYC.

Are you still in contact with other people who were students of Patsy?

I am in touch with many of my dance company pals via the miracle of Facebook. I adore Charlene Swayze. I text Cookie Joe and Nancy Schmidt regularly. I've had midnight chats with Sean, reminding him how much he resembles Big Buddy. . . .

We lost so many wonderful friends to AIDS. And it broke Patsy's heart.

TELEPHONE INTERVIEW: March 8, 2019

I think I saw in your email interview that you said you became a dance teacher because of Patsy.

Oh, of course.

Could you say more about that?

I think I told you that I became her demonstrator. I was thirteen when she moved to George Ballas' Dance Studio USA. I think she and my mother must have worked out a deal. I don't know this because it was never discussed with me.

I was to go straight from school on the bus to Dance Studio USA (which is where Patsy's studio was) completely dressed. I mean everything—bun, hat, etc.—to be her demonstrator. So we started out at 3:30 p.m. when the little kids got there. I just worked until my class. What this did for me was, it showed me how a teacher breaks down every little step: how they work with babies, how they work with middle elementary school kids, how they work with teenagers, even. I was at that age in her most advanced class. So I worked all of the classes under me as her demonstrator. So you can see that I gleaned a tremendous amount from Patsy. That's how she taught.

So fast-forwarding, I went away to college to be a ballet major, but I did not receive what was called the Norton Award, which was the scholarship for ballet. It was an expensive, private school, TCU (Texas Christian University). My parents did all they could do to send me there for one year.

So I just had to come back to Houston to go to U of H [University of Houston]. Patsy was the teacher at U of H. She really brought dance to U of H. Of course, now they have a dance department and everything else. Back then, she taught on the stage in Cullen Auditorium. Again, I was her demonstrator. So I had to go to U of H, dress up, and be there ready at the front of the stage with Patsy to demonstrate for her class. So you can see how she instilled teaching in me.

That very same year, that class gleaned a lot of college kids who wanted to continue outside of U of H. So she put me in charge of teaching that class at her studio. I guess you can say that was my first teaching experience with Patsy. And then she also got me a job with her friend Thaela McKeown, in a nearby town, Pasadena, Texas. And the name of that school was Twin Arts Dance Studio. Twin Arts is now owned by one of the students that I taught dance to at Twin Arts. The mother bought the studio and then the daughter took it over and now the granddaughter has it. We're talking a huge legacy from the fifties. Twin Arts Dance Studio is still in operation, winning championships all over the country. I mean, that's not from me, I'm just saying the school does really well. You can see that's how I got into teaching. I was with Twin Arts for quite a while.

And then a friend in Patsy's class at the University of Houston, a singer, approached me and said that a friend of hers was opening an art gallery/performing arts school and would I teach her how to teach. So I brought some manuals and worked with her for several weeks, and she finally threw in the towel and said, "Hey, would you consider teaching the dance side of this?" So I departed Twin Arts to go to this school.

Basically, I've been a teacher since college.

Wow. Are you still teaching now?

I had a private student. She's now graduated high school and gone on to A&M. . . . I worked with Shelby for probably three years. By the time she graduated the dance school, she was on point and doing very well. One-on-one private lessons can do so much for a person, especially when you're teaching Patsy's technique.

I also became a choreographer out of that. I founded my own dance company and moved to Florida and opened another dance studio. I had a freelance dance studio that catered only to daycare centers. So I was pretty active in the dance community.

I want to make a comparison. Maybe in all of the years I have taught dancing and all of the students I have had, which has been hundreds, maybe four of them have sent me a heart-felt note of gratitude. Patsy has thousands, thousands of people who admired her and thought she hung the moon. There is something so charismatic about this person that people just, you know, she changed their lives.

And maybe Rick Odums, in Paris, really follows in Patsy's footsteps. Cookie Joe has a high-functioning school. . . . She is so involved and raised money for our homeless shelter here in Houston. . . . She is quite an enigma, very much like Patsy. She is three years my junior, but she was in Patrick's class at Waltrip [High School]. So you have a lot of those kids. . . . like Teresa Lawrence and Emile Lawrence. . . . They come from a huge family, maybe fourteen kids, and Patsy taught them all. The mother did all of the seamstress work for the company; she created the costumes and was a very integral part of the whole picture. My point is the whole nucleus of where Patrick and l, and Cookie Joe, and Paula Tovar and all of those people were dancing together in Patsy's new company; many of those kids went to high school with Patrick.

I was lucky. I met Patrick four times at various events. In Houston, at the film festival where *One Last Dance* premiered, that's the one time I met Patsy. I only talked to her briefly. There were around a thousand people there, and she was speaking with a lot of us folks, the fans of Patrick. She just struck me as being so gracious, so nice.

Yes, she really is.

This is a cute story. Fans had flown in from Europe and all over the place to see the movie and meet Patrick and Lisa. Patrick and Patsy got on our tour bus and they spoke to us for about an hour. It was a surprise and we could ask them any questions we wanted.

You're kidding.

I was just lucky. I was in the third row. And of course, I asked a question. I was so nervous, so excited that I could hardly listen to the answer. It was just a really big highlight for me.

These are just down-home folks. . . . Here, we're not country, but it's just down-home family. All of us were treated the same as her children, basically, except they got a tougher road than we did. We were there with her so much. We were treated just like how you were treated on the bus. She's just a loving, kind person.

One of the fans on the bus wasn't feeling well and she had to get off the bus with her friend. And guess who looked after her? Patsy. "What can I do for you?"

She's really remarkable. When we lost her, our hearts were broken. I just can't say enough. So dynamic, just can't even put a spin on how dynamic this person is. Just would not let anyone fail. She would keep after you until you succeeded.

Would you say she was harder on her own kids than the rest of the kids?

Oh yes, absolutely. The daddy was military. When you see the pictures of them as boyfriend and girlfriend, you will see him in his military outfit. . . . So these are wartime folks. That generation was called the Great Generation. Of course, her mother would have been from the Depression. I had Depression parents as well. All of those folks were tougher than nails. You do what you're told. You don't talk back.

There was no talking back to Patsy. If we were messing around and not focused on rehearsal, she would stop the rehearsal right there. It was not to our advantage, because we had to be on the stage performing. When we were not in character for rehearsal, she would stop the rehearsal and give us a class, basically to punish us. In other words, *You're so bad, I'm stopping this class and working on your technique.* We were being punished by not getting to do our rehearsal for the upcoming performance. She had her way of telling us we were not doing what she wanted us to do.

But you know, as big as her personality was, it was big in all aspects. It was big in love, it was big in charity, and it was big in aggravation. She could get really aggravated at her kids. . . . Patrick had football injuries, but he was still expected to dance. . . . I'm talking about the sixties in the dance studio. . . . If he had been at football practice and his knees or his shoulders were bothering him, literally, she did not really care how much pain he was in. If he could work that hard on the football field, he could work that hard in the dance studio. Patrick was cut no slack.

Are you saying that she was tougher on him than his siblings?

No, definitely not.

Vicky won so many awards in drama. These kids were massively talented. It was her. People want to think it was them, but it wasn't, it was her. She is a driving force in all of us. She has people on Broadway. Right here in Houston, you may know about Playhouse Theatre. Playhouse Theatre was owned by Jim Mendenhall. Patsy choreographed almost every musical that went through Playhouse Theatre. Francie Mendenhall, Jim Mendenhall's daughter, was probably born on the property. Francie was there every single night for performance and in every performance and worked with Patsy as the choreographer. Same as Tommy Tune, except probably Tommy was at Playhouse Theatre and Theatre, Incorporated.

Just a little side note: Patsy was choreographing the last show that ever happened at Theatre, Incorporated. [Later] we stood out on the front yard and watched it burn to the ground.

Those two theaters in Houston were the pioneer theaters of this great city, and Patsy Swayze was the choreographer of both of those theaters.

When did this woman ever sleep or rest?

She didn't. When I was in high school, we may have worked until ten or 10:30. She would have puttered around, you know, picking up stuff, trash, or sweeping, or something like that. Then she would get home. As far as I know of Patsy, she was a late sleeper. She stayed up very late. She probably had to go home and clean up the mess in the kitchen or whatever. Big Buddy, her husband, probably would have gotten take-out or cooked or barbequed or something like that for the kids while Patsy was at the studio. So when Patsy got home, she had to do a load of laundry, whatever. I'm not sure what time she actually went to bed. If I had called her, it wouldn't have been unusual to hear a very sleepy voice on the phone at noon or one o'clock. That was her pattern. We rehearsed late. She was just a ball of fire. That's all I know.

I heard somebody describe her as a warrior woman. Would you agree with this?

Yeah, I think so. I guess you could say that. As far as warrior, the example I gave you of being in the very thick of the equal rights movement in the South, and putting a teenage girl, me, on stage with a young Black man. Being from Michigan, that's probably not so impactful—but down here, that was unheard of in the sixties. She was color-blind. She did not know color, race, creed, any of that. She loved everyone. She was a strong Catholic.

I think you wrote that she grew up in The Heights. What is The Heights?

Our city is so overgrown. It encompasses little cities inside of it. The Heights is like, I think it's an incorporated city of Harris county. It would have been a neighborhood that became a little city or a little town [located four miles northwest of downtown Houston]. The Heights, probably back when I was growing up, was not considered the place to live because it was older. It would have been one of the first communities. It was Victorian homes, so 1900. So as those homes decomposed and the neighborhoods decomposed, it was not the place to live.

But today, The Heights is all of the hip Millennial professionals—

very high-end professionals have bought the Victorian houses and restored them. So now The Heights is considered almost a historical monument; so many old, wonderful homes in there have been painstakingly preserved. So when I say she's from The Heights, some of the readers from Houston of course, or Texas, may know what that is because it's such a hot spot, such a cool place to congregate.

She did not go to Reagan High School, which is the high school in The Heights. Her mother insisted that her children go to Incarnate Word Academy of Houston. I don't know if all the sisters went there, but I know Patsy went there and graduated.

In 2002 maybe, the city of Houston had a gala honoring Patsy for all of her work and pioneering in the theater district downtown. When I was growing up, we had a music hall, which was a nice place to go hear the symphony and things like that, and we had the coliseum where you could see the Barnum and Bailey Circus and the rodeo and things. We took a turn into much more classy theatrical productions, largely because of Patsy Swayze. So she was honored. I sat at the head table with Patsy, the chairman and his wife of the University of Houston, her two grandsons, and two nuns who were two of her teachers at Incarnate Word Academy of Houston. So you see how important her high school was.

We talked about Marcella Perry, her teacher. I was determined to find out where Marcella Perry's studio had been. I found it in The Heights, right there on 19th. If you take Marcella Perry and you do an investigation about her, oh my goodness, now I'm talking about a house of fire. In the sixties, Marcella Perry went from being a dancing teacher to the president of Heights State Bank. Wrap your head around that one. Talk about a dynamic individual. So you can take Marcella Perry and compare Patsy. Of course, Patsy's mother seemed to be very dynamic as well, I'm sure. I only met her once.

Note from author: *Marcella Perry, 1907–1999.*

Pamela shared a story that Patsy told her about an incident that occurred when Patsy was living in Simi Valley, CA.

Did anyone tell you about the day she was working at the same studio as Patrick (in a different lot)? She was bent over, probably fixing someone's feet, when Patrick came up and said, "Mom, Mom. I want you to meet someone." She told me that she said, "Honey, I'm very, very busy. Not now." But he persisted and she looked up, and standing there was Elizabeth Taylor! Patsy told me this one herself.

FINAL COMMENTS: The biggest thing you can say about Patsy was she was an encourager. Patsy Swayze was my lifelong teacher, choreographer, mentor, and friend.

Cast of Characters

Sharks

Bernardo .... Tim Borquez
Chino .... Frank Cannata
Pepe .... Stephen Ruiz
Indio .... Joey Hembree
Jauno .... Bill Hastings
Toro .... Mike Pasco
Anxious .... Greg Stuart
Nibbles .... Frankie Rodriquez

Shark Girls

Maria .... Robin Klein
Anita .... Nikki Diane
Consuelo .... Janine Salluda
Teresita .... Tina Woodward
Franciscia .... Lisa Zulke
Estella .... Bambi Swayze
Marguerita .... Karen Mykytiuk
Paquita .... Lisa Arnold
Rosalia .... Nicole Gorsuch

Adults

Doc .... Howard Rogo
Schrank .... Paul Roche
Glad Hanna .... Marilyn McCormick
Understudy .... Teri Peterson
Krupke .... Wesley Hoggan

Courtesy of Michael Pascoe.

Program from the West Side Story *production by the Horizon Players in 1981. Photo to right: Top right is Nikki Diane (D'Amico) and bottom left is Michael Pascoe.*

WHO'S WHO

PATRICK SWAYZE (Tony)

Patrick Swayze has pleased audiences, peers, and critics through a long and varied theatrical career. Since moving to L.A. two years ago, he has starred in television movies for ABC, CBS, and NBC, with such people as John Ritter, Tony Randall, and Barbara Eden. He had critical success with the L.A. Times applauding his starring roles in the feature movie Skatetown U.S.A. and the award-winning production of The Brick and The Rose. Before coming to L.A. he starred on Broadway as 'Danny Zuko' in Grease, and as a soloist with the Eliot Feld Ballet Co. A theater background stretching from early childhood to All-American athletics has all added to the impact of Patrick's powerful, yet subtle style of acting.

ROBIN KLEIN (Maria)

Appearing for the first time on the Horizon Stage, Robin has had much success in the professional world of show business.

She has recently guest-starred in an episode of Taxi with Judd Hirsch, an episode of Dallas with Larry Hagman and was also in the motion picture Stripes starring Bill Murray.

Aside from acting, Robin loves to sing & dance.

DONNY SWAYZE (RIFF)

With a lifetime of theatrical background, Donny a professional draftsman by trade, is quick to adapt to any stage, including Horizon's, where he is making his simi debut.

With talents in Piano, Trumpet, Baritone and Harmonica, and in acting, singing and dancing, Donny has landed such roles as a featured Dancer/Singer in GiGi and also a dancer in Urban Cowboy.

TIMOTHY JON BORQUEZ (Bernardo)

'West Side Story' marks Tim's return to the stage after working in an original Jazz-Rock Band the past year.

Tim is a member of the Screen Actors Guild and has been seen recently in an episode of Fridays and a T.V. movie The Night The City Screamed starring Linda Purl.

Tim has done some commercial work and has been involved in well over 30 shows in the past six years in roles ranging from "Judas" Jesus Christ Superstar to Lead Dancer in Oklahoma.

Tim has performed in a local theatre group in Hollywood during the years of 1979 to 1980 and displayed his talents in Godspell & Two Gentleman of Verna.

NIKKI DIANE (Anita)

Born and raised in Houston, Texas, Nikki studied dance under director Patsy Swayze until she moved to Los Angeles in 1973.

Nikki has performed in both regional and professional theatre, the most recent being a featured dancer in the Los Angeles Company of Evita.

Her most recent film credit includes a dancing roll in the new Annie movie to be released sometime next year.

Nikki is returning to the Horizon Players Stage after a three year absence.

Courtesy of Michael Pascoe.

Who's Who in the program from the West Side Story *production by the Horizon Players in 1981.*

NIKKI DIANE (D'AMICO) Born and raised in Houston, Texas, Nikki studied dance under director Patsy Swayze until she moved to Los Angeles in 1973. Nikki has performed in both regional and professional theatre, the most recent being a featured dancer in the Los Angeles Company of Evita. *Her most recent film credit includes a dancing role in the new* Annie *movie to be released sometime next year. Nikki is returning to the Horizon Players stage after a three year absence.*

CHAPTER SIX

NIKKI D'AMICO

Actress, Singer, Dancer

Interview: August 2, 2020

Thank you for agreeing to do the interview. I recently spoke to Susie Ewing, Blake McIver Ewing, and Danny Ward. They said I have to interview you for the book.

Ah, nice. Patsy touched so many lives; that's the point. I mean, she touched *so* many lives, but my dealings, that's all I can speak of: my heart, my dealings with them, and for me they were truly like my extended family. . . . I treasure my friendship. I feel so blessed that I would have ever come into contact with Patsy Swayze. I owe it, of course, to my very amazing mom, who I actually just lost one month ago.

I am so sorry.

Thank you. I'm the youngest of three. My mom and I have that bond that's just unbreakable anyway. I owe everything to her, you know, the trajectory of my life that I started dancing school at two years old.

When you started dancing at age two, was it with Patsy?

Nope. I started dancing with a neighborhood dancing school. My mother saw that even at two years old, you know, when someone is like born with it, you just know it. I was so coordinated, even at two, the teacher took me on, but she was a little rinky-dink teacher. My mom knew of Patsy Swayze. This teacher was like a rival. For whatever reason, she kept me at this little dance school until I was eight years old. When my mom found out that I really had a great ability, she knew she had to further my learning. I always heard about Patsy Swayze. So she took me to Patsy, at eight years old [in 1960].

It sounds like you knew her from then until the rest of her life.

Until the day she died. She had many, many, many students while I was there. Many have gone on to Broadway [and to other wonderful things].

At eight years old, Patsy just took me under her wing because she saw my ability. As a child, I was very advanced. Back then, I guess you would say sort of like a little prodigy. I kind of caught up with myself. I just caught on to everything and Patsy saw my ability. I danced in every class from morning until evening and hated going to school. I would get out of school to go right back to dance classes. It's a wonder I ever graduated from high school. I lived and breathed dancing.

At twelve years old, because I excelled at ballet, Patsy took me and three of her older students (they were seventeen, eighteen years old) to New York City. I'd never been on a plane. I'd never been away from my mother and dad. And when we went to New York, the idea was that she would take us to all kinds of dance classes from other teachers, right? She took us to mini jazz classes and she took us to the Joffrey School. She took us to Harkness. Here's the thing: the other three students who were of the age where you knew they would grad-uate and go on to college, and try to start a career, nothing happened for them. But at twelve years old, I was singled out by Harkness and Joffrey. I was offered full scholarships to the Joffrey Ballet and the Harkness School of Dance.

Wow! What did you do?

So I came back home and, of course, I got letters from both schools. I could have gone to either one from the time I was twelve and lived there and studied until eventually, when you're like in your late teens, you go into their core de ballet of the company. Like I said, I was very close to my parents, and I loved Joffrey (just the little I knew about it). So my mother, God bless her, for three summers in a row took me to New York, and I studied at the Joffrey School from the most amazing teachers from eight in the morning until six at night, all different kinds of teachers and classes, and I got brilliant, brilliant training.

But at eight years old, I was introduced to musical theater, and that was truly my love. I didn't have the discipline to be a ballerina, but the fact that I ever went to those classes, it only made me a better dancer. So right out of high school, I always knew that I'd either go to New York or Los Angeles. Really and truly, I probably should have gone to New York, because my background was musical theater. But I came out to L.A. and I had a great career in dancing, doing all kinds of shows and tours. And then I tore my right knee ACL doing the show *CATS*.

Oh, no.

I studied with Patsy until right out of high school. She was the formative, major foundation of my career, inspiring me in every way to be a performer—to be a triple-threat performer.

I loved her with my whole heart and soul. I miss her to this day, constantly. I think of her and Buddy, and Big Buddy, and Vicky, the sister. I think of them so often. She and her family were such a huge part of my growing-up years. I am who I am to this day because they were such a huge impact on my life, along with my own family and the experiences I had. Patsy was my mentor and to me she's one of the greatest teachers there ever was. She just had that gift to teach. She was a brilliant, brilliant teacher and she gave away more classes than she ever got money for. She knew when somebody had super-talent for sure, but she could take anyone and just make them be the best they could be with what they had. Do you know what I mean?

Yes, I have heard that. It's amazing.
Do you have a theory why you think she decided to be a teacher rather than a performer?

I don't know why. She did some shows. I think probably she realized that was sort of her calling. She had children. I just think she was geared to be that, more than to continue a career. She got married very young, started having her babies. She was away doing what she loved, but also making a living. She's also a fabulous choreographer, as well, not only a teacher, but she was a super-terrific choreographer.

She sounds like she was a very busy woman.

She was a busy woman.

Patrick and Patsy, oh my God, they were so similar in so many ways—just their strength, both headstrong. They're very similar.

Is that why you think, out of all of the kids, Patrick became the quote 'star'?

No, I mean I think all of her children were extremely talented. Buddy excelled at anything he did athletically. First off, he and I dated all through high school. We did all of the musicals in junior high and high school. We dated in the 10th and 11th grade. I was in dance class the day he met Lisa, his wife [to be], and they were truly soul mates, in my opinion. Buddy had that born charisma. He excelled at anything and everything athletically. He was voted most handsome in high school. He did all the leads in the show musicals. He was a very well-rounded, super-talented human being.

And nice, right?

Oh, that's the other thing. He never ever, ever changed from the person he was. He never got caught up in that Hollywood scene [and] that was one of the other amazing things which set him apart from other stars. You never saw him in the rags, you know, those papers that say such awful things about people. He never was in scandals.

I think that is part of why he had so many fans.

I'm sure it is.

If you could talk to Patsy now, what would you say to her?

Well, you know, I saw her three days before she passed away. She couldn't talk. She'd had a major stroke. It was horrifying to see her like that. I told her then and there because I wanted to tell her while she was living, how much she meant to my life. I said how I just owed her so much for what she gave to me as far as her time, her energy, her love, her nurturing as a dancer, and her phenomenal gift of teaching, and what she meant to me as a person. I told her I just would always love her, which I do. Whenever I've been in a show since or do anything theatrically, there are so many times, I always say a little prayer and just say, "Patsy, this is dedicated to you." She's a part of me. She's a part of my being, for sure.

Oh, wow.

I loved them very much.

What else do you want to say about Patsy as a teacher?

She was all about technique. She really focused on technique, which really, as a dancer, is huge. You want to be technically correct. It really does set you apart from any other dancer. You know, you put two dancers side by side, and it separates the best from the good.

She also always stressed about being a triple-threat: to learn to sing, to learn to do acrobatics, to learn to do jazz, to learn to do tap, to learn to do ballet. She said to learn as much as you can so when you are called upon in a show or a movie—"Can you do this?"—you can say yes. She told us to be a triple-threat—actor, singer, dancer—and try to excel at them all.

That sounds like that was maybe progressive or different from a lot of the other teachers.

It was different because she was very well-rounded. She just kind of covered it all. It was about being the whole package, being a performer, you know, selling it.

What are you up to these days?

So like I said, in 1985, I was doing the show *CATS* at the Shubert Theatre, and you truly only dance at that caliber for so long without starting to injure yourself. I was a professional dancer for many years, and it was like a big transition in my life. I was already older. I tore my right ACL, which is a devastating injury for a dancer. If you were to continue—like say, if you were a ballerina—you would have to have it repaired. Being that I was older and I always wanted to be an actress as well, it was sort of like a blessing in disguise, in a way. It made me focus on the acting and the singing. I never had it repaired, to this day, knock on wood. I'm really working on my acting and I'm always studying. I'll always keep studying acting, off and on, I'll be taking acting lessons, but because of the way everything is now about COVID, nobody does anything in person.

At the moment, I am teaching Zoom Pilates classes. I got certified in Pilates in 2010. I separated. I was married for twenty-two years. I got divorced five years ago. Oh gosh, now what do I do? Because I am the sole breadwinner. I am definitely an *artiste*. I have no other skills but show business. I'm not teaching dancing because of the frustrations—not that I couldn't, but to not be able to fully do things I would want to because of the knee, it is too frustrating. Pilates is fabulous and it's so good for you. Knock on wood, I'm in really great shape.

That's super.
Do you stay in touch with some of the other people who were students of Patsy?

I have to be very honest. I am actually only in touch basically with Danny [Ward], now and then. We also grew up together in Houston. Honestly, the last time I saw the Swayzes was at Patsy's funeral. Sadly, I'm not really in touch with them. I mean, I'll see Donny in a commercial or something and be thrilled. I'm really not [in touch], but again, I love them dearly to this day.

Anything else you want to say about Patsy, or any of the family?

I was just like another child to Patsy. I was very close to Vicky, the daughter. They were like my second family because literally, I'd get up in the morning, go to school, and then the second I'd get out, my mom would take me there and drop me off and I'd be there for hours, all day long. Patsy would take me home. Our families were very close.

That's sweet.

This isn't to be conceited, at all, because like I said, she had so many students through her career as a teacher. I'm only one who came through her doors, but I will say for that time that I knew her, I was truly like one of her, you know, prodigy people. I mean, there were only two people that I knew of, and I will say that. Of course, once I left, then she concentrated on other people. I was one of the people she nurtured to really try to do the best, you know, professionally. . . .

If anybody at all in the Swayze family deserves to be written about and let the world know about, it is Patsy. It all happened because of her, for sure: her sacrifices, her love for the theater, just performing in general. She was, I'm sure, the inspiring force in Buddy's life, without a doubt, to live up to what she wanted for him. I think she was beyond tickled and thrilled when he became a star. In her mind's eye, she knew he would be.

I met Patsy very briefly in Houston at the premiere of *One Last Dance*. First, I spoke to her at the reception following the movie screening. Then the next day at a special event that the fan club organized, Patsy and Buddy came on our tour bus and stayed for about an hour to answer questions. I was super-impressed with Patsy and Buddy.

That's amazing. I love it!

She was just who she was. She did not mince words with anyone. She was the best. She was a great lady, a great teacher. I mean, who's perfect? Nobody's perfect, but oh, my gosh, in her profession they don't come any better, truly.

One of a kind.

Yeah, one of a kind.

I feel so blessed to have been born and raised in Houston, Texas and that my life's path crossed theirs. Let me just say that I'm a very spiritual person anyway and I believe there are no accidents. I'm so thankful. I loved my life growing up. I never wanted to grow up—*stay a girl forever*—and I still don't! My love for show business was because of her.

Courtesy of Nancy Schmidt and used with permission of Nancy Schmidt, Glenda Alexander, and Cookie Joe.

Tribute for Glenda Alexander in June 2019. From left to right: Nancy Schmidt, Glenda Alexander, and Cookie Joe (all dancers of Patsy) at Cookie Joe's Dancin' School recital at Jones Hall in Houston.

CHAPTER SEVEN

COOKIE JOE

Professional Dancer, Choreographer, Professional Dance Instructor, Director and Founder of Cookie Joe's Dancin' School, Philanthropist

Interview: December 11, 2018

When did you first meet Patsy Swayze and under what circumstances?

I was a dance student. I had been dancing since I was two at a neighborhood dance school. I'm Chinese and Irish-American descent, and in the fifties and sixties, there weren't that many kids in the arts. Most Chinese parents wanted their kids to be doctors and lawyers. So there weren't a whole lot of kids in my culture who took dance lessons. They could take piano because that made them smarter, but dance and wearing costumes and tights and stuff like that, that wasn't something that was encouraged by people in the Chinese community.

My mom, who is American, saw an audition call in the paper. They were looking for children of Asian descent. Of course, back in those days, they called them "Orientals." Like I said, there weren't very many of us. I happened to be a singer and a dancer, and I was nine years old, and so we went to this audition. It was for the part of the little girl in *South Pacific*. And it turns out Patsy was the choreographer. It was at a place called the Court Club, a very prestigious place. It was my very first show and it was a union show. It was amazing to have that kind of opportunity, you know, for your very first thing. I was talented, but I was not well-trained. I just looked right. So basically it was a real big case of typecasting. I went to the audition and I made it.

Patsy knew that I had been dancing my whole life, and she told Mom, "She's a beginner. She has never had any training. I suggest that, if she really wants to be in this business, she needs to get serious training." So at that point, I changed to become Patsy's student.

I was there the rest of my growing-up years. So that's how we met and I started going to class. And, you know, the rest is history.

Yeah. So you knew Patsy a long time.

Yes.

So after you studied with Patsy, you branched out on your own to have your own dance school and do choreography?

First, I danced professionally. We did a lot of children's television and also Houston had a strong theater program just throughout the city. So we did a lot of summer stock and theater work. Patsy did a lot of the choreography and sometimes it was other choreographers. We worked professionally the whole time I was growing up. I went to summer school every year so I could get out of high school early. I graduated at sixteen so I could move on—to my career.

So I danced everywhere. And then at about the age of twenty-four, I decided that I wanted to open my own school. Patsy was a big inspiration. I have followed in her footsteps because I have a dance company that is very well-known in Houston. We recently were featured [in the media], because we danced for President Bush twice! Since he passed away, we've gotten a lot of media and press over the fact that we were one of his favorite companies.

Wow. That's special. So Patsy was a big influence on you. What was it like to have her for a teacher?

She was really tough. She was challenging. She had high expectations of us. Her standards were very high. She was very different from any neighborhood dance teacher. She was definitely teaching people who wanted a career. A lot of her students went on to dance professionally or used their dance training in their work.

If you could speak to Patsy now, what would you say to her?

Mostly, thank you. I'm very grateful for the example she set. She definitely made it seem real, that it was possible to have that kind of dream, to have a dance company. I always wanted to be creative, to choreograph and produce and do shows . . . that were my concepts with my choreography, my costuming, my lighting. And because she did it, I knew it could be done. Watching her do it and watching her go through the process, I learned a lot.

I don't think she realized she was mentoring us. I think she was just doing her thing. We were just fortunate that we were like the little sponges watching her work and watching her achieve what she did. She was very creative. The message we got from her was that, if you can create and believe it, you can do it—"You'll find a way." That was a big influence on my IQ. There's just nothing I can't do. If I have a vision that I want it to snow or want to have a maypole flying from the top of the stage—you have to figure out a way to do it. She did not let anything stand in her way, and that's the influence and inspiration I've gotten from her.

I imagine that carries over outside of the world of dance and arts, into everything.

Absolutely. That's the way I train my kids: Pursuing excellence. I feel I can't make you pursue excellence, but I can try to encourage you to want to pursue excellence. And I think that's the message.

Also, Patsy was incredibly philanthropic. We give a lot for non-profits. And that's what my reputation is. I've raised hundreds of thousands of dollars for non-profits, like homeless shelters and cancer research, just from our productions.

The thing about Patsy, she was one of the real, first multi-cultural dance companies in the city. Being a bi-cultural child growing up, challenged with people who were always saying, "What are you?" and that sort of thing; there was never any feeling that there was a difference between any of the kids [in Patsy's classes]. We were all color-blind. It was all family. We were very close.

What about your contact with members of Patsy's family?

With Buddy?

Big Buddy, Buddy, and the other kids.

Well, the main thing was he [Buddy] and I were the same age. He was born in August and I was born in November, but we were the same age. We ended up going to junior and high school, the same schools. So we grew up very "sisterly-brotherly." You know, we were very connected.

Patsy's oldest daughter, Vicky, taught me how to wear make-up, how to put it on do it right not just for the stage, but also for teen-ager dating kind of stuff. She was a big-sister influence. Patsy adopted Bambi, and being Asian, that was a connection for us. We understood the culture and it made Bambi more comfortable having more Asians in the family when she was adopted. So that was also a big thing.

Sean was a baby at the time. I can still remember him running around in a diaper, in the studio. And Donny was younger than me and we went to the same schools. I'm in contact with his kids today. We do events together now.

Growing up in that family, spending social time together was also part of our experience.

How about Big Buddy?

Big Buddy was wonderful. He was the glue that kept that family together. He was always at the studio, always laughing, always smiling. He was a great example of what a good father and good husband could be. He was just always loving, and sweet, and kind. We just loved him.

So all of Big Buddy and Patsy's kids were taking dance?

Well, not really. Even Buddy didn't take class very often. Buddy came to class when he could use his muscles and lift girls. He was not big on enjoying the actual experience of doing all that hard work on stage. I think as he grew up, he appreciated her art form more. He did gym-nastics and skating, and his football training, you know, that was more of what he really liked to do.

But out of all of the kids, he became the star.

It was interesting because I do not think he was even looking for stardom. I think he just really liked hanging out, playing music, doing sports. He liked riding his horses. So it was interesting that he would end up being so high-profile.

Did Patsy ever talk about why she became a dancer and her training?

She would always tell us when she was younger, she used dance as a therapy. She'd been injured. Basically, those stories about having to walk through the snow: she was letting us know how much she had to sacrifice to become the dancer she was. That was part of the legend, so to speak. . . . What I am saying is basically giving us the example of how hard it was to for her to achieve her goals, 'cause she started out at a disadvantage. You know how older people say, "I had to walk through snow to get to school?" Well, hers was, "I had to come back from such severe injuries."

Patrick sort of did the same thing. He came back from a lot of injuries: the knee injury, the football injury.

Yes, he did. And also he got a severe staph infection at some point, so that was really difficult.

Even with his illness, he never gave up. And that's I think kind of a testament to his strength of character and strength of bazillions—that he never wanted to give in or give up.

That was very amazing, very amazing.
What else do you want to say about Patsy?

I think one of the things that I learned so much from her is about encouraging kids to go all the way, encouraging them not to be satisfied with [being] mediocre. She always made us go to the front. We weren't allowed to stand in the back. We weren't allowed to be the back-row person. There are no wallflowers. We had to be very much front and center, because she felt if you worked this hard, you want to make sure that you're seen. Sometimes, it's easy to try to be invisible when you feel insecure. She would always tell us, "Shake it 'til you make it. Make sure to go for it, no matter what." That's our personality now. I think my kids today feel that same way.

The interesting thing is that when I see my kids dance, I see Patsy in them. I see the generations; we still are following her footsteps in style, in technique. You can tell a Cookie Joe dancer immediately. Everyone tells that me a Cookie Joe dancer is a Patsy Swayze dancer. . . .

Patsy taught me to be a triple threat. In other words, I'm able to teach any style of dance. There is no, "Well, I'm just a ballet teacher. I'm just a jazz teacher." She encouraged us to do everything. There's a lot of great ballet schools, a lot of great jazz schools, hip-hop schools, but I'm one of the few schools able to teach any type of dance. The fact that my kids can do anything, so any time an audition comes up, I have the dancers that can fulfill those requirements or those requests, because they're all so diverse and well-trained. And that is intentional.

I'll tell you one of the neat things that happened that I think was very divinely orchestrated. Once she moved to California, Patsy and I did not talk that often. I did visit her a couple times, but I called her. I don't know, I was running through my phone, and I saw her number, and [thought] I'm just going to give Patsy a call. She was already eighty-six years old and blind and retired. I called her and said, "How are you doing?" And we talked. She was dead within two months from that day.

Oh, my goodness.

I will always be grateful that I took that opportunity to call her. It was just very off-the-cuff, "I think I'll just give her a call." I was very blessed and very excited that it accidentally happened. Of course, I don't believe in accidents. I believe that I needed to talk to her before the end. So I was not able to go to her funeral and be part of it because, unfortunately, I had shows to do. I was still doing what she taught me to do—that the show goes on. Patsy would want me to stay home and do my shows. So that was a deciding factor on why I stayed home.

Anyway, as I said, if I could say one thing to her, it would be: Thank you! And also, I would be saying, I hope you are proud of me. I hope she sees how much influence she's had on me and that she sees that I have taken her legacy and vision and continued it, in trying to honor her and making sure that we keep it going.

The cool thing is that I've got kids who want to continue it after me. I am sixty-five now and one of my students is thirty-five, and she's now my partner and will continue the vision after me. Our school will see the hundredth anniversary, because I'm at forty-three years now, and I still have twenty years ahead of me. So I have no doubt that someone will celebrate the hundred-year anniversary of that school.

That is really wonderful, especially in the type of world we live in today. Arts aren't always emphasized much.

And the thing about me—I think it's my Asian background—is being independent and being self-sufficient is part of my deal, not depending on other people. We self-promote and self-finance our own dance company. So we have a non-profit company, but our school profit business supports it. So I'm able to pay for production and costumes and everything through my school, to support my non-profit.

And as I said, we've raised hundreds of thousands of dollars for people: children in need, senior citizens, and the military. So we make sure that our name is connected to the words: service and compassion. And that's something that Patsy would have wanted.

Yes, I think so. I think she would be proud, if I'm allowed to say it.

I appreciate that. Thank you.

You are welcome.

The thing is what makes me really happy is that Donny has said it. The fact that Donny feels that way, that means everything. Donny's wife, Charlene, did an event for an all-abilities park, and I participated in it and I donated money so we that could have a bench, a memorial for the Swayze family. They sent me a rock that Buddy used to wear around his neck, just to have something [that is] part of his heritage and his legacy. The families will continue to be connected for years to come.

Yes.

I met Patsy once, for about five minutes in Houston. It was a film event for *One Last Dance*, when that premiered, and then Buddy and Patsy got on our tour bus and answered questions for a whole bus-load of people for almost an hour.

Oh, wow!

It was really a great experience. I was just so impressed by Patsy when I had a chance to talk to her. It was under five minutes I'm sure, just a one-to-one. She seemed so humble and gracious, "Thank you for coming," that type of thing. I didn't know what to expect. It always stuck with me.

I think she was gracious, but I mean that woman was a woman of power. She was a warrior woman and that's what I take away from it. I am a warrior woman, too. I have been through two different hip replacements. My father died in my arms.

I'm sorry.

I had this autoimmune disease and doctors before told me I shouldn't be dancing and working this hard. And yet, it's like: "Get out of my way. I've got a job to do." I think she instilled in me that same feeling. "You just do it." That's how we feel.

Francie Mendenhall (center), along with her brother Mendy Mendenhall, hamming it up during rehearsal of their offstage Christmas caroling for the 1959 Playhouse Theatre production of A Christmas Carol *(starring Robert Foxworth).*

Francie Mendenhall with Pat O'Brien in the Playhouse Theatre production of The Loud Red Patrick.

CHAPTER EIGHT

FRANCIE MENDENHALL

Actress, Singer, Performer, Former Original Dean Martin Golddigger

Interview: May 19, 2020

You sent me your bio. I was just wondering, if before we get into your connection with Patsy, you would like to talk a little bit about what it was like performing at the age of seven at the Playhouse Theatre in Houston.

Okay. I can't say my upbringing or my life as a child was ordinary, but when you're a kid, you don't know. I mean, that's just what's happening. My dad was part of this theater, the Playhouse Theatre. He was a leading actor there and became the producer and managing director, and produced and directed many plays and musicals. There was an instance when they needed some kids. My brother and I were asked to sing off-stage for *A Christmas Carol*. Robert Foxworth was playing Scrooge.

Oh.

Yeah, a lot of talent in Houston. They say, "What was in the water there?" So we did a lot of children's plays, *Peter Pan*, oh, just reams of children's plays. And then *The Loud Red Patrick* came along with Pat O'Brien. They had a season using stars, and it was a family show, and they needed someone like me. I loved it. It was wonderful. I had to have my hair dyed red. Going to elementary school, it's like, "What did she do to her hair?" "Oh, her picture's in the paper! Oh, she thinks she's so *ooh*." But, you know, it was all fine. I was different. I was totally invested in the theater from that age on. I barely made it to school, but I did graduate. That was my childhood.

I went to New York with my dad when my parents separated. He had a summer stock company in the Catskills. I went up there and then went into Manhattan with him. I was hired by *The Patty Duke Show* to be one of the kids in the classroom.

I loved that show.

I came back home to Momma and continued. Marietta Marich and her husband had taken over the theater and renamed it the Houston Theatre Center. And Marietta really was the one who championed me. Going back to Patsy—Dad had done a really wonderful production of *Gypsy* starring Marietta Marich, and Patsy choreographed it. My brother was in the show as one of the newsboys. I was too young for that show, there was nothing for me. But I was there at so many rehearsals and got to know Patsy and met her daughter Vicky, and just loved her.

Later on, before I went to New York with my dad, I was in a production there of *Carnival* that Patsy choreographed. It was so much fun. She wanted me to do this part in the show where Lily, the main character, is mesmerized and dreaming of her future. A figure is up on a rope twirling very, very slowly. Patsy chose me to do that, so she took me to some place out in the country—it was where circus performers rehearse. Someone taught me how to climb this rope: wrap my hand around this loop, and then someone at the bottom would hold it very taut, and I'd take one leg and press it against the rope and then the other leg to do like an arabesque and arch a little bit.

How old were you at this point?

Twelve. That was great.

And then I met her son, Buddy (Patrick). He decided I was just the bee's knees, and asked if I'd go steady, and I said, "Sure." So then I don't think I saw him again. I can't remember what area of Houston they were in. We were twelve. Then this boy in the show decided he liked me too, and I thought, *I am really confused.* I am going to tell

Patrick that I can't be his girlfriend. Later on, I saw him when he was here in Houston honoring his mother Patsy at Theatre Under The Stars. Once I reminded him who I was, he looked at me like, "See!"

That's cute.

Patsy gave love, in abundance. She was a very strict teacher and she commanded respect, which was gladly given. She was just a fine teacher with a fine background. The best guidance I have ever gotten would be from strict teachers and mentors who had great talent themselves.

I think I first met Patsy when I would have been like eleven. I probably was thirteen by the time we did *Carnival*. It was so much fun. I left then to go see my grandma in Iowa and then to my dad in New York and then came back to Houston to Mom. But, you know, Patsy stayed in my life. Also, when I got back from New York, I had missed a few months of school. I got back in school and Patsy wanted to offer me dance classes for free. She was so kind. My mother was supporting both of us in a small apartment at that point and she knew all that. I went there and took classes from her, just about every day during the week, I think.

She taught me one thing that really has nothing to do with performing. She taught me how not to spill sugar when you're trying to put it in your coffee cup: Don't move your hand, you move your body, pick up the sugar, keep your hand still, move your body, dump the sugar. It works perfectly.

Anyway, I always ran into her, and we kept in touch. When I auditioned for the Golddiggers, she was there. It was at her studio; that was the place to be. And then I went on to do that.

Note from author: *Francie clarified that Danny Ward knew Patsy and played piano for her audition for* The Dean Martin Show *at one of Patsy's studios in 1970. They have been friends ever since then.*

Later on, I came back to Houston to audition for *The Best Little Whorehouse in Texas* and again, it was her studio where Tommy Tune and Peter Masterson held the auditions. We kept in touch, like family; we always wanted to keep up with each other. Phil Oesterman—another one of the clan there, was a very talented director—who we have lost now.

I'm sorry.

Thank you.

Phil was taking charge of a Tommy Tune production, *The Will Rogers Follies*. A gal was leaving the show and Patsy told him, "You need to hire Francie." I talked to Phil: I mean, he's like family, too. He directed *Peter Pan* when I was a kid, and was Tommy Tune's best friend, and was around during *The Best Little Whorehouse in Texas*. His understudy of the role had been waiting and waiting for her chance to take over the role of the wife and I know he was pulling for her. He was sort of pleading with me. I turned down the opportunity for the role in *The Will Rogers Follies*.

Phil always reminded me of when we were doing *Peter Pan* and I played a mermaid in one of the scenes and I had on a mermaid outfit. We [mermaids] were carried and laid down so we would be there when the lights came up. And then when the lights went down, we were picked up and brought up the aisle. Well, one day, nobody picked me up. I was inching my way up the aisle, when the lights came up. At notes after the production, Phil asked, "Francie, why were you still in the aisle?" I said, "It's because nobody struck me."

Note from author: *Francie explained that "struck or strike" is most often used in the theater for taking props or set pieces away, usually in the dark or during what is called "a blackout." In this case, a mermaid in the aisle was considered a "prop."*

We talked about that when I was in my thirties, when Patsy's tribute was at Theatre Under The Stars. I think it was in the early 2000s.

What do you remember most about Patsy?

Her wonderful smile, her warmth, her generosity of spirit, and her humor. I remember doing a plié in class. Again, I was young and I did not have a filter. I said, "But this is so unladylike." I mean, it *was*. I don't know if you know what a plié is: your legs are apart and you're squatting down.

Anyway, she was full of joy. She thought that was hysterical.

If you could talk to her now, what would you say to her?

I would say, "I love you Patsy. Thank you so much for teaching me and being my friend. And I miss you. Hope you're dancing all over heaven."

That's sweet.
So you've talked a little bit about your contact with some of the other family members, with Buddy and Vicky. Anybody else?

Big Buddy, oh yeah, he was a sweetheart. I was at the house a few times, you know, sitting around the kitchen table, just like family. He was again a very warm presence. Patrick's younger brother, I met him at the tribute. Patsy had adopted a child who I never met. I was out of Houston at nineteen, so I missed all that.

You're there now, right?

Yes, I am back in Houston. I came back and stayed with my mom, and she's gone on, about five years ago.

I'm sorry.

Thank you.

There's a lot of history here, but I am certainly not as competitive as I used to be.

It seems like you are very active, including performing.

Yeah, I am. It's just different.

Oh, what a lovely time. Also, Patsy gave enthusiasm and confidence to everyone. She would walk around to each student during their warm-ups and give individual notes to each one. It was just wonderful. She wasn't out there with a baton yelling—she was very hands-on, gave very individual treatment in a classroom setting, in a dance setting.

It sounds like you formed some bonds with some of the other students.

Pam Mistrot [Rost]. I think actually her mother was the one who gave me a ride to the classes, so Pam and I got to know each other and we were both going to Lanier Jr. High. We've been friends ever since.

We were running buddies there. We used to go back to my apartment and iron our hair, you know, like Twiggy, put on the really pale lipstick and the dark eye makeup. We were so cool.

Pamela is a fantastic dancer. She was in Patsy's company. I'm sure she's told you.

She did.

Her other students, I mean I've known Cookie Joe since she was a little bit. She was in one of my father's productions of *South Pacific* and just precious. She was in shows with Marietta Marich as well. Marietta was/is very well-known in this town. Marietta had her own television show here. She was a singer and a wonderful actress. She would mentor artists. She could do everything: design sets, build sets, act, sing, and teach. She mentored me more than anyone.

Tommy Tune once said that there is something that people in theater do before the show, especially before opening night. They all gather back stage and hold hands in a circle and pray and then with one big shake of all the hands, they say "good show!" One time, Tommy said, "Our circle is getting smaller." Those people who were there for decades and decades and understood the same joys and grief. So what do you do? You live on. You look up and say, "Thank God." I'm not saying it was always easy. It never is. Anyway, I have wonderful memories. Somebody bought the building. I haven't been able to go inside. It looks totally different and I don't know; it looks all tattered. There was history there. It was the first theater-in-the-round in the United States.

When was that do you think?

In the fifties. Mr. Rosen designed and built it. Herbert Kramer was the first artistic director there, and when he was ready to retire, he passed it on to my father, Jim Mendenhall, and his partner, Mitzi Wayne, and their third partner, Bert Weil.

They both starred in shows for Herbert for most of the fifties. Then my dad and his partners started to produce and direct the shows there, in the late fifties and early sixties. They did so many wonderful productions of plays there, before they started doing musicals. *The Fourposter* was one. The author, Jan de Hartog, came to town to see the play. Later it was made it into a Broadway musical re-named *I Do! I Do!* starring Mary Martin and Robert Preston. Oh golly, so many shows.

My father, Jim Mendenhall, had the stage rebuilt from a rotating theater-in-the-round to a bastard proscenium—it means it was not totally uniform. He produced *Gypsy, Little Mary Sunshine, Call Me Madam, Li'l Abner, The World of Susie Wong* (I don't think it was a musical.) So many! Then Marietta went on to do almost all musicals, except she did one Dylan Thomas play that my dad came back from New York to direct.

She used me in *Carnival* and then *Brigadoon*. I was fourteen or fifteen at that time, understudied the lead, and I got to go on one night. It was incredible. Then I had a role in *Stop the World, I Want to Get Off*. She starred me and the first love of my life, David Doty, in *Half a Sixpence*. I was sixteen. He was seventeen.

We did reviews, which were very popular when Dad had the theater, and we continued them with Marietta. They would call them the "champagne reviews" and they were on New Year's Eve. You'd see the play and then afterwards, you'd see the review. It was all wonderfully talented people like Larry Hovis, who went on to work on *Laugh-In, Hogan's Heroes, Right for Wrong*, and many, many game shows. He came back and was one of the leads in *The Best Little Whorehouse in Texas* for Peter Masterson. He was brilliant. My dad did *Come Blow Your Horn* with him, and it was a great production. Oh, so many.

So many memories.

So many!

Just to go back a minute, you said the Playhouse Theatre was bought by someone else. It's not a theater anymore?

It *is* a theater. It's called The Museum Theater. It looks like it is shut-down. The billboard says, "Call this number for reservations." One time, my brother stopped by there and met the man who was running it. He let my brother inside. My brother told him the history of the theater and told him, "You know, you really ought to get this registered as a landmark"—which has been done. I went by there a year or so ago, and indeed, it has been registered. It's a Houston, Texas landmark.

What else do you remember about Patsy?

If she saw something she didn't think was right, she would say so. If somebody had said something or done something she didn't believe was proper, you would hear about it. I just love her. She was always full of joy.

I was really happy one time when I was living in New York. She came for something with Patrick. She came up to my apartment and I invited some people over who wanted to see her. At that point, I had hardly any furniture. She came up, and everybody surrounded her and talked to her. It was a wonderful reunion.

That's sweet.

Yeah. I think that was the time I was there in the late eighties.

Going back a little bit, you said when you were around twelve, Buddy said something about going steady, but then you didn't see him again.

I went to school and I did the show. I went home and I went to sleep. I went to school. I did the show. To my knowledge, he was not in the theater anymore during that time. He had given me his disk, which was the thing you did at the time, with his name on it—you know, something to wear around your neck. I really struggled and I felt really weird 'cause we had said these things to each other. We hadn't even kissed. We were so young. This other boy who was in the show with me wanted to take me out and go steady and give me Valentine's candy. I started feeling extremely conflicted, so not able to handle the stress. I told Buddy I was going out with somebody else.

And what did he do?

I don't know. I gave his disk back to his mother, I think. It was kind of, "Do you want to go steady?" "Sure." "Okay, see you next year." I don't know what that means, except you're sweet on somebody.

FINAL COMMENT: He was so gorgeous, and such a wonderful dancer, and such a sweet man.

Used with permission of Deidre Russell.

Deidre Russell.

Used with permission of Deidre Russell.

Deidre Russell (front row, far right) at Patsy's dance class.

CHAPTER NINE

DEIDRE RUSSELL

Professional Dancer, Choreographer, Dance Teacher, Registered Nurse

Interview: August 30, 2019

When did you first meet Patsy?

I had been taking [lessons] from the Margo Marshall School of Dance, and then they moved too far away and she gave my mother a referral. So I first met Patsy when I was eight years old, when my mom signed me up. Mom and Patsy were talking about classes. I had never taken jazz before, and Patsy was telling me all about it. She like demonstrates, too, 'cause she's just that way. I thought, well, it looked like a good place. My mom signed me up for lessons.

Age eight. That is something. At that point, did you think you wanted to be a professional dancer, or was it more of a hobby?

From the time I was a real little kid, I knew that's what I wanted to do.

Were there other dancers in your family?

No. It's kind of weird. My mother played piano and sang. I don't know really where I got that idea.

So how long did you know Patsy?

From age eight until she died.

What did you learn from Patsy, and how did she influence you?

Oh, my gosh. I spent more time with her than I did my own mother, as time went on. I learned things like joy and hard work. You can do anything you set out to do. I learned respect and teamwork and how to be a good person, and how to make your mistakes and then work hard to rectify them. Pretty much everything a parent would teach.

Were you dancing every day?

When I was eight, I think I took [classes] three times a week. By age ten, I was dancing pretty much every day. I got my point shoes at age eleven, and then by that time, I was every day. You know, she had a company, the Houston Jazz Ballet Company. They worked off grants. She had a fabulous reputation in Houston. She paid us by the show, like some years.

Really.

Yeah, like some years. And we went on tour all across Texas and Louisiana, and all the way to Florida.

Wow.

The unbounding energy.

She had it, or she taught you to have it?

She had it *and* she taught me to have it. She was like, "Of course you can do that!" The thing about Patsy is that she just believed in you so much, that of course, you did it.

Is there anything else you would add regarding what you remember the most about Patsy?

Well, Patsy let my boyfriend—who she never even met—come out and live with her for two months in L.A. before I could come out and live there. If you were family to Patsy, you were family, no matter what. That just meant everything to her.

I'm sure she went to church when she could. She had a deep faith. She did not believe in abortion. She believed in the sanctity of life. And if you were family, that meant, I am here for you.

Patsy also said dance is a giving art. My mother asked, "Why do you want to be a dancer? You just want to be adored on stage or something?" Patsy said that it is a very giving art. I know that because, when I was on stage and got an ovation or something [I felt] we've shared something and brought something to people. In that moment, you are together in like creation and everything that is good about the world.

So your mom didn't really approve of you being a dancer?

No. She gave me lessons, but nobody in my family wanted me to be a professional dancer. They wanted me to go to college, meet a nice man, get married, and have a family.

Couldn't do both?

It's pretty hard to do both.

Because of the hours and dedication it takes to be a professional dancer?

Right, and the travel, and so forth.

I was lucky to do it for seventeen years. I owe all of that to Patsy. She was pivotal in getting me out of my shyness. She taught me to think positively about the world, have a great work ethic, and be honest.

She could motivate a rock to get up and dance, sincerely. And she was very truthful, too.

Do you ever think she was abusive as a teacher (not that anybody in connection with this book has said this)?

I never saw her lay a hand on anyone. I did see her sit in a chair and just hold her head in her hands and look miserable after we did something wrong. "Oh, for Pete's sake, come on, what are you all giving me?"

No, the fact of it was, is, she's great. I think that's what we need today. No, she was not abusive in any way.

She never called anyone out and she never put anyone down. She built people up. She expected that of course, you are a good, honest, hard-working person. She refused to believe anything less than a hundred percent of what you could do. And that's the kind of person you will work for.

I think I credit her for all the positivity and can-do attitude I have.

If you could speak to Patsy now, what would you say to her?

I remember when I went to the retirement home where she was, this was just like a few months or a year before she died. It had been a long time since I'd seen her. I said, "Patsy, it's Deidre." She replied, "Well, you don't look like her."

I would just tell her, "Thank you for all that you taught me, and what can I do to help you?" She fostered that in me. She told me that I was a sweet person.

Once, I even brought my little boy and we stayed for a couple weeks at her house out in L.A. She told me, "You have to have a sterner voice with him." But she loved him and liked how he played and stuff like that.

It's like what would you say to your mother: "I love you so much. I'm so glad to see you. Thank you for being there for me, and all the things you gave me."

It just sounds like you had a beautiful relationship.

She, to me, in my mind was my second mother. I don't think I would have grown up to be the person I am today without her. She taught me about life. She didn't sugarcoat stuff. She told us exactly what it would be like to be a professional dancer. When I grew up and became one, I saw exactly what she said. I was prepared. She loved us.

There was a group of people that she mentored, right?

There was the original group that I came in on the tail-end of, and then there was my group and then there was I think another group after that—plus all of the people she mentored when she had a studio in L.A.

That's very amazing.

I'd see her get tired. I'd see her weather stuff through her family. She was a dignified person with a deep faith, and just by example, she showed you how to weather stuff.

What contact did you have with any of her family members?

Well, you know, everybody took dance except for Sean. He would run around the studio. My little brother would play with Sean. I remember they would play marbles, and sometimes the marbles went into the studio and you had to watch out.

I remember when she adopted Bambi. She did one of those Christian children's fund things where you send money to help a child in a different country. They wrote her a letter and they said, "We regret to inform you that we think your daughter may have mental delay." She said, "She is not mentally delayed. I've seen the pictures she's drawn. This child is fine. There's nothing wrong with her. How dare you say that!" So she put into place whatever it took to get her formally adopted and brought her over here.

Bambi came over when she was four. It was discovered Bambi had an ear problem. You know, today they put tubes in kids' ears when they have an ear infection. She probably couldn't hear most of the stuff going on when she was a toddler. She became an honor student, bright as a tack, and a beautiful little dancer. So here's Patsy saying, "You've got to be wrong. I've seen how she writes to me and the pictures she sends me, and this child, there's nothing wrong with her!" Sometimes, if she was going to be late doing something, they'd let Bambi spend the night with me at my grandmother's house.

So I guess I knew all of them. Vicky was a little bit older than me, so I didn't really pal around with Vicky. I knew Donny, who was my same age.

Patrick was a few years older. He was so good-looking, and such a great dancer. I'd be all shy around him. So I wouldn't consider myself in his circle.

And then Bambi. I'd spend so many hours there, especially rehearsing and stuff, that I kind of just considered them as like brothers and sisters from afar.

My mother got mad one time because I was there so late. I don't think it was a school night. Well, that's what you do. It's like if you want to train for the Olympics, or if you want to train for anything. In a dancer's life, you have to do this when you're young, when you are a child. You don't go to college and become something in four years.

It takes like a good ten years at least, or more. And you have to do it when you're young.

What about Big Buddy, Patsy's husband?

I used to think he had to be a saint because Patsy would be spending so much time with us. You know, I lived with them for about three months in L.A. before I could get my own place. He was kind of like a salt-of-the-earth guy. To me, he was a very positive person. He loved Patsy. I know it must have been hard for her to have all of that, you know, the dance studio and be there for everybody else. I think I went over to their house a couple of times when I was young, too. I didn't really sit down to talk to him until he was older. He just seemed like he was like a kind, good-hearted person. I never saw Patsy and he fight or him yell at anybody.

Do you have any theories why Patrick was the kid who became the star?

Well, I do. Patsy said if you're born with a good facility—like you're born with the feet and legs and body that you can make into a dancer—and then you have the work ethic. You know, a lot of people are given a lot of things, [but] they don't have the work ethic because they're not used to working hard to get something. And if they don't have the stick-to-itiveness, they just fall away. I think that's probably true in any profession, where only one out of a thousand actually get to do it. You have to have the mental ability and the body for it, and the work ethic. And Patrick had all of it. He had a good physique and a good work ethic and he had excellent training with his mother. And he had the attitude of stick-to-itiveness, and never give up. You put that together, and a person will be successful. You have to have [the whole] package to be able do it. Patrick had the body, the mind, the work ethic, and the training. And he loved to do it.

You know, he was supposed to be a ballet dancer. He had a football injury. Patsy said, "Go out for everything." You know, some people say, "Don't go into your sports at school, only concentrate on dance." Patsy said, "If you can play football, great, play football!" But then she would be mad because his muscles would be all tight from football and he had to stretch out again. He got the knee injury in football. It was not going to be in the cards [for him] to be in a company. He did go out for the Harkness Ballet in New York, first thing.

Patsy told us all, "To be a success in this business, you should be able to do ballet, tap, jazz, you should sing, you should do acrobatics. Do it all." So that's what he did. That's why he's a success. If you had Patsy for a mother, and the desire, and the physique to do it, I don't see why you wouldn't be a success. And also, Patrick was a nice guy.

He seemed that way.

He was. He was a really nice guy. He would go out and have fun and pull stuff. He was just a nice person. Patsy raised her kids to be good people. You know: Don't lie, don't steal, don't say bad things about people, work hard, mind your own business.

I met Patrick very briefly a couple of times at events. He was super polite. He seemed like he had a good sense of humor.

He does. That's all her kids. That's how you're supposed to be. He was funny.

He and I were pas de deux partners before Lisa came in.

Really.

I was like twelve and he was sixteen or something. She would pair people in class and have us do really hard lifts that you don't even see performed very much today. I always felt safe with him. You know, like one hand assemble lifts, where you're being lifted over his head with one hand. An arabesque where you're lifted over the head with the guy's hand underneath your arm pit, and the other underneath the inner thigh of your arabesque leg.

I knew that he was always paying attention and doing what he needed to do. Patsy was right there. I always felt very safe. When a person more his appropriate age came in, they just looked so good together. He paired Lisa with him.

There is some funny story. I don't know if it was Donny or Little

Buddy [Patrick] . . . They used to play by the railroad tracks near their house. My brothers did that. You know, people look at the trains when they're going slow and kind of jump on, and when it goes fast, you jump off. One of them jumped on the train and it went fast and [he] couldn't jump off and ended up in Galveston.

Oh, that's funny. Buddy talked about teaching other actors in *The Outsiders* how to train-hop.

Maybe it was Buddy. That's what I was told. I can't say a hundred percent that it was him. I do know that both he and Donny used to do that. I just don't know which one of them ended up in Galveston.

I guess he was just raised, you don't sweat the small stuff, you know, look at the overall picture, and what kind of person you are inside. I credit Patsy for giving me a really good foundation about that. You want to bring other people up with you.

People say that she was in an accident and she started dancing for therapy.

Oh, my gosh, that's right. I think she just got mesmerized by the life. She described it as such a giving art, like you were sharing so much. If it wasn't for you sharing this stuff, people would never get to see it or feel anything—contrary to the "I'm so great, everybody's clapping for me" kind of thing.

Buddy would talk about wanting to give people something through being an artist.

That was like one of the foundations of Patsy. . . . I think that is one of the most important things about Patsy that she gave to people who she mentored.

Are you in contact with other people who were mentored by Patsy or her other students?

Mainly on Facebook, because we are all so spread out. Mainly Zetta [Alderman], Doreen Levin [Laurie], and of course, Donny.

Bill Chaison taught me at High School for the Performing and

Visual Arts for a while, but he has passed on. Glen Hunsucker, I took [lessons] from him as an adult. He was one of her students. He had a big studio in Houston and taught a lot. A lot of people took from her at some point. Ron Abshire also taught at High School for the Performing and Visual Arts. He took from her a couple of times. I think they were in the era before I got there. She taught so many people that it wouldn't be unusual for a lot of people who are dance professors or in the business, to have taken from her at one point.

It sounds like you could go into the thousands.

Oh, I'm sure. And then you know, she taught Jaclyn Smith. I'd see photos of Jaclyn Smith when she was fourteen at Patsy's studio. Tommy Tune took from her. I'd see pictures of him in the studio books.

Of course, there's John Travolta.

Oh my God, yeah! John Travolta was really skinny and shy on the set of *Urban Cowboy*. Pretty much, anybody who took from Patsy could be in the group scenes, if we wanted to. I went to one of those group things where everybody was doing the Cotton Eyed Joe. The Cotton Eyed Joe is a country-western line-dancing kind of thing. It was filmed at a disco close to the Galleria area, not at Gilley's. I do know that they did film other scenes at the real Gilley's.

Someone was telling me they were paired up with Scott Glenn.

Zetta was in it. She actually got a part in it. She played somebody's girlfriend. Zetta was a good dancer. She was one of the younger crowd. Like I said, there was an older crowd, I got in on the tail-end of, and then there was me, my crowd, and then a younger crowd. Leath Nunn and Zetta came in later, back when Patsy shared a space with Chris Wilson, who taught acting at University of Houston. Patsy taught at University of Houston for a time.

Leath went on to dance ballet for his whole career and then he had a dance studio in New Jersey. . . . He was somebody who had taken gymnastics. He took from Patsy and became a beautiful dancer.

She could just take somebody if you had the work ethic and the will and the desire, you will be a dancer.

Is there anything else that you want to say about Patsy?

I guess it's just that she extended this feeling of family for all of us; that we were all working together for something. If someone fell in class—in a lot of places, if someone falls, people laugh—oh, she would cut that down in a New York minute. Or if she found that anyone was gossiping about somebody; that just did not occur at her studio. She would cut you down until you felt like an ant and then tell you that she expected a lot better out of you.

Patsy would tell you if you did something wrong. She might yell, but she never put anybody down, and everything she said, that I knew of, was right. Like if you did something, if you talked about somebody, you were lazy, or you lied about something. I mean you had to do something wrong to get Patsy to yell at you.

You know, you just hear stories about dance teachers.

Oh, no, no. But she wasn't like the coddling type, either. If it didn't look good, she'd tell you. It was always like, "I expect better of you. You're capable of better. Why are you not doing it?"

The only time Patsy would get mad was if she thought you were not coming up to what she thought you could do. And she knew; she had a really good eye. She could coach people who you thought could never really dance into being dancers. She never shamed people, like another [person] shamed me.

Are you still dancing?

I still teach ballet. I'm sixty, [and] you can't dance professional ballet at age sixty. I still take class during the summers because during the year, I'm teaching. I choreograph and I coach dancers in variations for Youth America Grand Prix [YAGP].

Note from author: *From the YAGP website, "Youth America Grand Prix is the world's largest global network of dance. It fulfills its mission of dance education through scholarship auditions, master classes, alumni services,* *educational and outreach activities, performances, and films."*

I had a dance studio for ten years. After my divorce, I went back to school and became a registered nurse. I'm a registered nurse and then I teach ballet normally twice a week, and then as it gets closer to variations and stuff like that, I'll go four times a week.

You are busy.

It's all very normal, because if you're able to do it, then you should do it. Actually, I credit my upbringing with Patsy for that. Be a good person and work hard. Give to other people.

There were some things I saw her weather. I know she loved her husband, and in her mind, when you get married, that's it. And they really did love each other. I know they went through a couple of problems, but Patsy just weathered it all and so did Buddy. They were a great couple.

I was raised by a single mother, so I really liked to see that. It was actually Patsy's family that brought me up with the values that I have.

She touched so many lives and was a pivotal influence. And those people went on and gave to other people.

So in a way, it's still her going on.

As famous as Buddy got, it really should have been Patsy. He was a beautiful dancer and a completely wonderful, talented person. Her story deserves to be told. . . .

I saw Patsy teach people from all over, different backgrounds. . . . Patsy always had a rainbow of colors in her studio. I had a friend whose mother wouldn't let her take [dance] at Patsy's because it was so integrated. Patsy was integrated before any of this became, you know, a buzz word. She would take you from any background and it didn't even occur to her. She never thought about anything other than: What kind of person are you? Can you dance? And then [she would] build you up.

Was Debbie Allen around when you were there?

No, she had left. She was in the older group.

There was like very disparate backgrounds at that studio. When we were all there, nobody even gave anything like that a second thought. We were all a family. I guess that's another good thing about her. You could have been from the worst background in the world, but it didn't matter a bit. We were all a family who worked hard together. I think that was very beneficial. She just cut through all of that mess.

That's cool.

I probably wouldn't have had the same upbringing as I did, so many different people from different economic and social [groups] and skin color. It was like we're all together and we're all family and we're all working hard. We each have our problems.

Dance is a way to work out your problems. If you had some kind of family strife you were dealing with, well then use it for class. You can convey something; you can bring that into your own ability to share and dance and give to the public in a positive way. Take your sadness, take your shame, and take your despair—okay great, well then you can use that in *Giselle*.

Used with permission of Deidre Russell.

Deidre (middle student in back row of the class)
taking a dance lesson from Patsy.

Used with permission of Nancy Schmidt.
Nancy Schmidt, from the seventies.

Used with permission of Nancy Schmidt.
Nancy Schmidt and Buddy Swayze.
Love Story, January 1973.

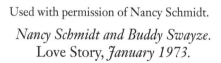

CHAPTER TEN

NANCY SCHMIDT

Professional Dancer, Teacher

Interview: May 31, 2019

When did you meet Patsy and under what circumstances?

I met Patsy when I was about eight years old [in 1964]. I was dancing at another dance studio and a friend of mine there, Glenda Alexander, had moved over to Patsy's. So I went with her over there to visit and meet Patsy. I really liked her. My mom moved me over there to take classes. It was a more advanced studio than where I was.

How long did you take dance lessons from Patsy?

From eight years on—I mean, for my whole life. Basically, I was in touch with her my whole life.

I was teaching up in Colorado later, in my thirties, and she came up and did a master class.

Wow.

I moved from Texas to California before she did, probably around when Buddy and Lisa did from New York. So I spent the first Christmas there with them. Then Patsy came out a few years later and she opened up a studio and I substitute taught for her at her studio.

What did you learn from Patsy? How do you think she influenced you?

One of the main things she always implemented in all of us, I believe, was work hard and you can accomplish your goals—just don't do it half-way. You can always do it better.

When we were in the dance company, the Houston Jazz Ballet Company, she would always make us understudy all the roles. I always made it a point to step right in there, even though I was real little. A lot of times she would say, "You're too little. You're too little."

Oh.

Well, I was. I was small. I still am. I'm only five [feet], two [inches], but I knew everybody's roles; so when we had rehearsals and somebody was missing, I could always jump in. I always took that to heart. One of the first things she told me was, "You are going to have to work really hard." She pushed hard, but she got great results.

Did you ever think she pushed too hard?

No, I don't think so.

You hear stories, not about her, but just about dance teachers in general.

No, nothing like what you see on TV now. She's not like that.

What do you remember most about Patsy?

She was like a second mom to me. I spent more time at the studio than I did at home. My parents had a business. I remember my mom going straight from school, dropping me off. I dressed in the car and put my tights and leotard on, and I stayed at Patsy's until ten o'clock at night sometimes.

Did you know when you first signed up for dance lessons, when you were around eight, that you wanted to be a dancer?

Yes, I was three when I first started. My mom always wanted to be a dancer, so she put me in dance, and I loved it. She put my older sister in dance too, but my sister hated it. I always wanted to be a dancer. I went to Performing Arts High School there in Houston. Patsy helped to get that started, as well. I was in high school and I just did the bare minimum because I was going to be a dancer, that's all I was going to do. In my senior year, my father told me, "You have to take a typing class, in case you need to be a secretary, 'cause you can't dance the rest of your life." Which was a good thing, you know.

Yeah, that's all I ever wanted to do was dance.

So after you finished at the Performing Arts High School, what did you do next? Did you go to college? Did you start teaching dance then?

I wasn't going to go to college 'cause my family [members] were not college people back then. Women got married, you know, in the fifties and sixties. I was going to go with Disney on Parade, because another dancer that danced at Patsy's was my boyfriend, and he went off to that, along with Buddy. They were both on tour with Disney on Parade. So that was my big dream, to go there. And then I was going to go to California.

Disney on Parade didn't pan out for me, because there was like one opening and people came from all over the United States. I didn't happen to get it. But anyway, Patrick came home and then we danced together in a lot of lead roles, *Raymonda Ballet* and different things, before he left for New York.

I got married, not to a dancer—and that did not last—so I ended up going to California and dancing out there.

I taught for Patsy out there and then I auditioned a lot and did some dancing out in California. The guy who was my boyfriend was in Colorado and he wanted to open a dance studio there. He had started teaching. He invited me to come open a studio with him. And I was close to his mom; she was like another mom to me as well. I moved to Colorado to open a dance studio there. I taught at Colorado for five years and danced with a local company there, and did some choreography and things. Spring City Ballet is where I taught there in the Pueblo Arts Center.

And then?

Then I went to dance with the Oregon Ballet.

This had been your lifelong passion. Did it feel like your dream came true?

Not as much as I would like—because again, I was always pressured into the "Oh, women get married." I'm sixty-three, so that's what women were supposed to do. Then I lost both of my parents.

It wasn't easy for me in the sense that, you know, it just fell into my lap.

Right. All of the hours that dancers put in; that's a lot of discipline.

A lot, yeah.

What do you remember most about Patsy?

I remember her being tough, and she loved us. And I remember when she had her studios in Houston—again, this is in the sixties—there were a lot of Black kids I went to school with who did not dance. She'd take a Black student and teach him at the High School for the Performing Arts, and then she'd bring the student to the studio. And the students excelled so quickly. She would take someone who was a non-dancer and make him/her into this fantastic dancer in a very short period of time.

Wow.

She was very talented that way.

I know, like Rick Odums is in France and he has a company there and he's been knighted or something by the French government. Very successful dancers. A lot of them went to Broadway. I just remember she was one of the best teachers in Houston.

She was very generous. For a while there, I was her assistant with her company. I did a lot of the stuff at the studio, taking in payments and stuff like that. Half the time, she didn't even charge people. Most of the kids, she didn't charge. She never made a lot of money. She could have done very well, but that wasn't her goal. Her goal was to make dancers and make them good.

If you could talk to Patsy now, what would you say to her?

I miss you. And thank you.

Are you in contact with any of Patsy's family?

Yes, I used to have contact with Buddy and Lisa in California, for a little while, until he got real famous.

I'm in contact with Ricky in Paris on Facebook, and Cookie Joe. She has a studio there in Houston, very successful. She's wonderful. Pam Rost or Mistrot . . .

That's how I got to you.

Yes. . . . I mean, there's like batches of students, they grow and they leave, they grow and then they leave. I guess they had a reunion, but I didn't get to go to the reunion. I think I was living in Oregon at the time. So a lot of them now know each other. There were several generations of studio people. I think I stayed with her through several of those.

Wow, several generations.

Just different groups. The original ones in the company were Pam, Cookie, and Kim Freund-Burkhardt. There was a group before me. Paula's sister, Candace, was in New York, on Broadway. We met her one time [when] I went with Patsy on a trip to New York. She took a bunch of us to a dance convention. She was a member of the dance association. There's Dani . . . I don't know her last name now. And then Lily Wong, she's in New York now. I don't know all their married names. They're on Facebook.

There are so many people. It's cool.
What do you remember the most about Patsy's family?

Big Buddy, her husband, was like a daddy to everybody. He'd always come in the studio and we would all run over. I remember Sean, the youngest boy, he'd come screeching through the studio sometimes. He'd slide in on his knees. I remember Donny. I grew up with Donny.

You grew up with Donny?

Well, he was younger than me. I was between Patrick and, it's hard for me to say Patrick, we always call him Little Buddy. But I know most people know him as Patrick. So I was between Little Buddy and Donny. And then Sean was younger. I remember when Bambi was adopted from Korea. Her name was Bora Song when she first came to the studio, and she named herself by pointing to the deer, Bambi. She was reading the book.

Oh, is that how it happened?

She was always reading the book, *Bambi*. So they named her Bambi. I remember her walking in, when they first brought her.

She's a fantastic dancer. Oh, my gosh, Patsy molded her into a really beautiful dancer. Well, they were all good. When Patsy choreographed *Urban Cowboy*, Donny was my dance partner throughout the filming of the movie.

You were in *Urban Cowboy*?

Yes, we all danced with Patsy. Zetta Alderman had a speaking part. I grew to know Cooper Huckabee, and his girlfriend, Mary. She's still my best friend.

Note from author: *Nancy shared that Patrick came to the set of* Urban Cowboy *to visit a couple of days after he finished filming* Skatetown, USA.

I heard Patsy had really done some intensive teaching of the two-step to John Travolta.

Patsy was there teaching all of them: John Travolta, Debra Winger, Scott Glenn, Cooper Huckabee, and all of them. I partnered with Scott Glenn at that time, only as a teaching partner.

What was he like?

He's a method actor, and once he went into character, he became that character. Before that, we had the dance lessons, so I got to meet him that way. Years later, I was in Sun Valley, Idaho. We walked into a restaurant with some other people, and I said, "Oh, that's Scott Glenn." I didn't think he would ever remember me, and I walked up to the table, and I said, "Hi Scott." And he goes, "Hi Nancy. How are you? I'm getting ready to do a movie with Patrick." It was that Wild Bill movie . . . .

Tall Tale?

Yes. It was funny. He introduced me to his wife and his daughter. I was like, wow, he's got a good memory. I didn't think he would remember that.

I was just thinking about Patsy's family . . . Vicky, just before she died, she was out in California, too, so we talked quite a bit. She was a great choreographer, but she's a beautiful singer, a beautiful voice.

Very talented.

Yes, all of the kids were. Sean's the only one that never went into dance, the youngest boy.

Do you have any theories on why Buddy turned into the kid who became the big star?

I think he wanted to please his mom. I think he wanted to thank her for everything. I think he pushed himself. He always just really pushed himself hard. I remember an interview he did one time and he said he never felt like he was accomplished enough or was good enough. I think that was something he strived for. I don't know if that had anything to do with his mother, but that was just something that drove him. He was very driven. He was very athletic. So I think that's what pushed him to go further and further.

He had all of those struggles with his knee.

Yeah, since high school. I remember we would be in rehearsal or dancing and he would just like squinch in pain and limp off. We did a lot of partnering together. I know he got frustrated with it and he would get upset and walk out because he was hurting.

I know he had several operations. I think at the end there he was okay and I know that's why he switched from dance to acting. And his brother, Donny, is a very good actor.

Is there anything else you want to say about Patsy?

When I was teaching in Colorado, she came up and taught there, so we were always in contact. She always had kids that lived with her, a lot of students.

Really.

I know Lisa did. Ralph Hamilton lived with her for a while. She would just take us with her, wherever she went. So she kind of adopted us, I think. She looked at us as *her* children, you know.

One thing, I remember, [and] I find myself doing it with my kids. I still dance around the house. When the music would start, it would just make her move, when she was choreographing or teaching class, she'd move. To us, she was forever young. As I have gotten older, I'm like, wow, she was this age.

Yeah.

So those are just spots of memories.

Very vibrant, very energetic.

Right.

She was a wonderful lady, that's all I can say. I am blessed to have been a part of her life and have her in my life.

I met Patsy very briefly in Houston and was really impressed by her. It was 2003, when they had the premiere of *One Last Dance*.

Note from author: *Nancy said she wondered how I knew about Patsy and if I had met her. I shared the story that I told Pam Mistrot Rost in Chapter Five about the events at the screening of* One Last Dance, *which included the question and answer session on our tour bus with Patsy and Buddy. Then I told her how I developed a "connection" with Buddy, which had led me to meeting Patsy.*

***Dirty Dancing* just really resonated with me. I had become a really big fan after the 1988 Barbara Walters interview of Buddy. Then I found Buddy's international fan club online and I joined and then Buddy came to Detroit, twice with Complexions [2002 and 2004]. I had a chance to talk to him just a little bit.**

The fan club was a really cool group of people. I'm still in touch with Margaret, who was president. Buddy and Lisa always kept the club informed as to what was going on professionally. I wrote two books on *Dirty Dancing*.

You did?

I did. And then I wrote a third book about Buddy. I met so many people by writing these books. Also, it's always interesting to me, you know, families, and how did somebody turn out this way.

So I was just really touched by Patsy, even though I only talked to her personally for maybe three minutes at the *One Last Dance* premiere. I wanted to learn more about Patsy and honor her.

I think if she was living, she would be blessed by someone writing a book on her.

Do you think so?

She's the one who was the driving force and made all these people who were successful dancers, and I don't think she got enough credit for it. She adored her son. He was so talented. And she really loved to see the kids succeed at their dancing. When I would visit her when I was in California, she'd start talking, "Well, Lily is doing this, and so-and-so is doing this, and so-and-so is doing this." She'd keep you up to date on everybody. She was very proud of their accomplishments.

When Buddy became so famous, she just fell into the shadows. I don't think he would be who he is today without her. I thought that might be a little sad for her. I don't know for sure, but I know she was proud of him. She always enjoyed the accomplishments of her students. I don't think she received the accolades that she should have for being the teacher she was.

How many people do you find like her these days?

You don't.

I just find it stunning, just remarkable what Patsy was like. . . . I tried to research her earlier, actually, before I even thought of doing this book, and there was not that much stuff on the internet.

I think she was more in the shadows. She created a lot of famous dancers in her time. They got the recognition, she didn't. . . .

When did you last see Patsy?

I guess when she came to Colorado. I was teaching at the Pueblo Arts

Center. That's not the last time I talked to her. I'd usually call her on her birthday.

Sweet.

Yeah, I think we all did. . . . most of her students. That was the last time I saw her in person because I had left California and went to Colorado and then I went up to Oregon. When Facebook came around, then I got in touch with a lot of people.

There is a scholarship fund set up in honor of Patsy at the dance department at the University of Houston.

I danced in the dance department at the University of Houston. I went there.

Most of the people I knew, they are no longer with us. I mean, some of them are. Of course, like Cookie. She's a couple years older than me. Cookie is wonderful. She's been very successful. I think she models her studio after Patsy's. She was in the original group, and Pam, too. I think Pam was eight when she came to Patsy's studio.

FINAL COMMENT: I think she deserves this book.

Courtesy of Jessie Mapes.

Don Swayze on the set of the movie Urban Cowboy.
He was an extra and Nancy Schmidt's dance partner.

In Simi Valley in 1986. Front from left to right: Leanna Sparacino, Buddy Swayze, Lisa Niemi, Bambi Swayze. Back: Rick Odums, Patsy Swayze, and Sean Swayze.

Above: Leanna at age 22 at Patsy's studio on Ella Boulevard.

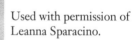

Left: Leanna and Bill Chaison dancing in 1967.

CHAPTER ELEVEN

LEANNA SPARACINO

Professional Dancer, Choreographer, Instructor, Producer, Director

Interview: July 16, 2019, Update: January 11, 2022

When did you meet Patsy and under what circumstances?

I went to audition for the Houston Jazz Ballet Company, the junior company, when I was ten or eleven years old.

Wow. And you had a successful audition?

I did. I had a successful audition. The first year I was there, I absorbed everything like a sponge and I loved Patsy and everything she was doing. So I worked my tail off. When the older company would stay for rehearsals, and the younger dancers went home, I stayed and watched. I learned quickly and was the body when they needed someone to fill in, "Can you go stand over here or do this?" So a year later, I was accelerated up to the main company.

I danced with Patsy until, well, even after I was an adult. When she moved to California, I would go out and work with her at her studio, and then when she traveled to teach in different places, I would go with her and demonstrate.

I was active with her up until probably about the last five years of her life, and after that we just visited with each other.

You actually saw her during the visits?

Oh, yes. We stayed connected up until the time of her death.

That's like a lifelong friendship, mentorship.
So was that the first time dancing, when you were ten or eleven, or had you been dancing already?

I started dancing when I was two-and-and-a-half years old.

So you always knew you wanted to be a dancer?

Well, no. My mother started me when I was young. She was a product of the Depression. She always wanted to learn dance and never could. So when I was a little girl, she took me to a studio. Patsy's studio was in our neighborhood, and there was one other studio. For whatever reason, Mom could never connect with Patsy's studio. You know, that was long before answering machines, so I ended up at the other studio.

Right.

And then I kept reading about Patsy and her group and what she was doing. When my mother found out they were having auditions, she took me. So it just sort of happened and I just never quit. I loved it and still love it. I still dance to this day.

That's wonderful. Are you teaching as well?

I teach full-time. I also perform periodically.

You are busy.

Yes, I have a ninety-four-year-old mother that I help with and a four-year-old granddaughter that my husband and I keep regularly.

What did you learn from Patsy? How did she influence you?

She really helped mold my life. I spent as much time at the dance studio as I did at home, maybe more. I learned ethics and morals. She really helped shape my life, besides my craft (how I've earned my living all of these years), how to be a good person.

What do you remember most about Patsy?

She was a very strong, independent person. She did not hold back for anything. You knew where you stood with her at any given moment.

If you could speak to Patsy now, what would you say to her?

I would tell her it was a joy having her in my life. I am the woman I am today, largely because of her. I miss her and she is always in my heart.

The last time I talked to her, I just told her how much I loved her and how much I appreciated everything she had done for me. By this point, she couldn't really talk. She was literally on her deathbed. We were on the phone. Do you know her niece, Stormie?

I know of her.

She was there with her. She made sure my call was taken and that I could speak with her.

That was a very bad year because my father died in March and Patsy died in September. So I lost my father, and then six months later, I lost Patsy. That was a very hard pill to swallow. They were a tremendous loss for me.

I am sorry.

It has been almost nine years and there are times I still forget they are gone.

**That was a very connected relationship, very strong.
I am really hoping to honor Patsy with this book. That's my goal.**

She deserves it.

I had a chance to meet her in Houston at the premiere of *One Last Dance*. I was a big fan of Buddy. Members of Buddy's international fan club came from all over the country, and even from Europe, for the movie screening. . . . That was the opportunity I had to meet Patsy. I only talked to her for about two minutes that night. It was really special. I wanted to know more about her.

Long before she was Patrick Swayze's mother, he was Patsy Swayze's son.

What contact did you have with the rest of Patsy's family?

I've had close contact with all of them. And I was at the premiere that you were referring to, with Kitty, Patsy's sister, and Jimmie, Patsy's nephew. We went to a reception before the premiere. I don't know if it was the one you were at?

No, it wasn't before the premiere. We were just at the general reception after the screening of the movie.
Buddy made a point of having photos taken with of all of us at the premiere. The next day, Buddy and Patsy, got on our tour bus and we had a question and answer session. It was a surprise arranged by Margaret, president of the fan club. It was great!

The whole family is very down-to-earth. We were at the studio in Houston on Judiway, probably in the 1960s. The place had a swimming pool. It had previously been a nightclub; so it had a huge room where we had rehearsals, a large wardrobe room, and office spaces. There was a bar, not really an alcoholic beverage bar, but a food bar. It had a patio, and the pool. We had a trampoline. When we weren't dancing and rehearsing, we were either jumping on the trampoline or swimming. I knew Patsy also taught swimming lessons, although I never took any from her.

Stormie, Jimmie, and their brother, Michael, and their little sister, Wendy (she was a lot younger), were always there with Buddy, Donny, and Sean, before Bambi was adopted. So we were all just a very closely knit family. Everybody was down-to-earth and I could pick up the phone and call any of them today.

Nancy Schmidt, Mario Durham, Diane Smith, and I were all about the same age. We all got to be very good friends. . . . Some of my fondest memories are from this time with these people.

There are multiple generations of people that Patsy raised. When we were at the studio, she had all these eight-by-ten photographs up above the mirrors and all around the room. They covered everywhere. I grew up looking at the likes of Tommy Tune and Jaclyn Smith and Debbie Allen. Farrah Fawcett was up there. The list just goes on and on and on. All of these people were working professionally. I might be going out on a limb, but I don't think there are too many areas of the entertainment industry that she did not affect in some way.

That's a good point.
***Urban Cowboy* I think was the first film she did choreography for?**

Yes, that was several generations later.

I think that a lot of what you will encounter when talking to people is that they were either part of this time period or that time period, but not many of them traversed all of the time periods. That was one of the benefits I had of staying with her lifelong.

Yeah. Wow.

She just didn't touch one part of my life. She touched all aspects of it. We were together through many stages of both of our lives. I was with her here in Houston. At one point, well two different times, I lived with her in California.

I know at one point, she was very involved with a theater in Houston called Theatre, Inc. It was long before my time.

She encouraged all of us to learn everything we could about dance.

All different types of dance?

Jazz, ballet, tap. She would bring in different teachers from around the world: prima ballerinas, and Russian dancers, and Hawaiian dancers.

I had not heard this before—that she had teachers from all over the world come in. That's awesome.

I have a drawer full of pictures, records, and I even have the check stub from my first pay check as a dancer at eleven years old.

So she became a dancer because she was in a car accident and it was therapy, and then it sounds like she must have just really connected with dance. So it wasn't like she came from a family of dancers.

Oh, no. Her sister, Kitty—the mother to Stormie, Jimmie, Michael, and Wendy—was a singer. She and I kept in touch and visited regularly. She lived in nearby Baytown, Texas. We stayed in contact until she died.

When did she pass?

Patsy was still alive. You know, time is flying. It's hard to keep up. Kitty passed away in 2003.

I found it striking that Patsy passed away almost on the date in September that Buddy did. It was three days apart or something. I don't mean in the same year.

Do you know about Vicky, her daughter?

Yes.

Patsy took that very hard, as any mother would. But I think after Buddy also died, it just kind of killed her soul.

That's a heck of a lot to go through. There are no words really.

Yes. She also lost her husband, Big Buddy, too soon. In the end, Little Buddy was really the one that kind of took care of her. As wonderful as she was, she didn't have any business sense.

Her husband, Big Buddy, had done all of that earlier on.

Yes, and then after he passed away, I am not sure who took care of it in the interim before Little Buddy took it over. She did require assistance in that area.

Do you have a theory as to why Buddy became the star, out of all of the kids?

Well, he was more outgoing, personality-wise. The others were more introverted. He was out there. And she had all the connections. I think he just enjoyed it more. Buddy was always there. He was happy there.

Bambi was a dancer, too. She was in *One Last Dance*.

Yes. When they adopted her, they brought her to the dance studio and she was always there, so she was in class. She grew up there. She was very good, too. Now I have not had much contact with her in the last twenty-five years.

What else do you want to say about Patsy?

Well, something that might give a little clue to her personality. One of the funniest things I ever saw her do. We had been to an event in L.A. On our way home, she was driving and we pulled up at a stoplight. The car next to us had their hip-hop rap music on so loud, that our car was vibrating from it. She liked to listen to classical music in the car, and so she said, "I wonder what they'll do, if I turn mine up?" She turned it up. She cranked it to the top. I was cracking up. I don't even know if they could hear it. It was like, "Listen to this, buddy, you think you got it?"

That is hilarious.

She was funny. We traveled to lots of places together. She liked to sleep with the TV on and the lights on. And that's the one thing about the whole family that always drove me nuts. None of them require much sleep, three to four hours and they're good to go. Me, I gotta have eight. I like the dark and the quiet, so when we traveled together, that was always an issue.

Three or four hours, that is not a lot of sleep.

I guess that's how they accomplished so many things.

What an amazing family!

They are indeed. Like I said, just as nice as they can be, down-to-earth, and always helping people.

Lisa came into the picture when we were about eighteen.

She was a little younger.

She is probably close to my age. I'm younger than Buddy was.

FINAL COMMENTS: Patsy was very passionate and she was a very good motivator. You knew when she praised you for something, she meant what she said. She was just as likely to tell you that you look like a skeleton, as she was to tell you that your lines were gorgeous and your jump was six-feet-high. When she told you something was fantastic, you believed her.

Note from author: *Leanna shared that she danced at the memorial for Patsy. She also accepted The Dance Houston Legacy Teaching Award on behalf of Patsy in 2016 (see image). The program for the award ceremony states: "PATSY SWAYZE: Thank you for training and inspiring a new generation of dancers." Leanna also shared that Patsy was honored at the Eighth Annual Lehman Awards at The Alex on November 12, 2000.*

Used with permission of Leanna Sparacino.

Patsy, Buddy, and Leanna in the 1990s.

Cover photo courtesy of Ad Deum Dance Company, *Bitter Earth* choreography by Steve Rooks.

Program cover for: Dance Houston's 14th Annual Celebration of Dance, November 5, 2016, The Wortham Center. Honoring: Mary Martha Lappe, Mitsi Shen, Patsy Swayze.

CHAPTER TWELVE

DANNY WARD

President, Ward & Ames Special Events

Interview: July 10, 2020

When did you meet Patsy and under what circumstances?

I met Patsy because I attended Black Junior High School prior to attending Waltrip Senior High School, and my background is that of being in music. It's a long story, but I play piano. In junior high school, I ended up playing for all of the theater class Broadway show rehearsals, and that's where I met Buddy Swayze. And then there's another important part of this and if you want somebody else to interview: Nikki D'Amico. If you google Patrick Swayze and Nikki D'Amico, you'll see photos of them. They were the male and female leads in all of the Broadway shows through junior and senior high school. So I met Patsy through affiliation and friendship with Buddy and then Nikki. She lives in California and is still a great friend of my wife and me. She's just a super person.

There were a couple of other dancer folks, [including] Cookie Joe, that go back as far as junior high school. I got to know Buddy and Nikki, I played for choir rehearsals, played for theater rehearsals, and I was in the band. I was a music nerd in junior high and high school.

So then going on into high school and being a friend of Buddy's, I can't actually remember the year but I think it was sixty-seven (I graduated in 1971), I started going over to the studio on Judiway. Patsy Swayze's studio was this amazing place. There were trampoline lessons. There was a swimming pool and swimming lessons. There were classes of all kinds. I just remember Patsy and her amazing style helping students, dance classes of various types. It's hard to pigeonhole somebody. To me, she was like a female Bob Fosse, so caring and so wanting to see the kids do well. I actually was a lifeguard at the pool. I played piano for the dance classes. I was friends with Buddy. I was over there a whole lot in my junior and senior years in high school.

As a senior at Waltrip Senior High, I was the drum major of the band when Buddy was the star of the football team. Then I think, as you know, he injured his leg. That's my story of getting to know them and friendship with Buddy. The last time I saw him after we graduated high school, he got on his motorcycle and rode off, said he was going to New York.

Subsequently, he came back here in the eighties. So my wife and I are in the production of special events. Buddy raised Arabian horses here. We did at least one event where Buddy sang. In fact, Larry Gatlin came in to sing "Ride Like the Wind" with him. We maintained friendship. We were invited to the film premiere here, and so was Nikki.

Was that for *One Last Dance*?

Yes.

I was there.

Oh, really. What's your story? Are you from here?

Note from author: *I recounted how I became a fan of Buddy, meeting Buddy in Detroit twice at Complexions Contemporary Ballet events, and meeting Buddy and Patsy in Houston at the premiere of* One Last Dance.

Maybe you were there at the reception after the movie?

I was there. Absolutely.

The experience in Houston was really special and I'll never forget it.

Well, I do understand.

So then back to Patsy. Patsy Swayze, with the way she was able to inspire her students, many of them went on to Broadway. I've got a list around here somewhere of which ones ended up going. There was an occasion, I think it was '68 or '69, there was a summer replacement on NBC for *The Dean Martin Show* called *The Golddiggers*. In fact, the Golddiggers were an ensemble that I think were on some years on *The Dean Martin Show*. Greg Garrison actually came here to Houston. Patsy asked me to play for the audition. So I played for, I can't remember other than Francie [Mendenhall]—beautiful Francie—and a couple of other girls actually got the job from that audition. Francie still lives here, and we occasionally touch base with each other, a really nice person.

I knew Big Buddy, Buddy's dad. He sort of ran the operation there on Judiway: the dance studio, the pool, and everything that was going on. Kind of a quiet guy.

I just can't say enough about Patsy and how kind and inspirational [she was], and she was positive. She was strict, but she inspired, as far as I'm concerned, a lot of these dancers as they went on to careers, some of them after taking lessons at the studio.

We also were involved in our business. I guess the most famous Catholic hospital around here was St. Joseph Medical Center (and since then it has changed hands). So we did an annual event. Patsy was honored one year. We put together a group of some of her students to do some dance performances in her honor.

Beautiful. When do you think that was approximately?

Late eighties or early nineties.

Did you know any of the other family members?

I loved Buddy's sister, Vicky. She was just great. I'm so sorry about her pathway.

Bambi danced at the event that we did. In fact the event, I just remembered, was at the Great Southwest Equestrian Center. It was a horse show. Buddy sang. Larry Gatlin sang. Bambi danced. Gosh, that was also quite a long time ago.

Was it at a big arena?

Yes, a horse arena.

Buddy came out riding a horse. I have seen a video of the event. What do you think inspired you the most about Patsy?

Her positive attitude and the way she inspired her students and encouraged them. At the same time, she was tough. She brought the best out of her students. Just a kind smile and always a dear friend, whom I stayed in touch with for many years, even when she went to Simi Valley.

Do you have any theory as to why Buddy became the star out of the children?

The cream, you know, comes to the top. He was handsome, chiseled. He was the guy who took dance lessons and he was also a football player. Chiseled in terms of being very muscular and masculine, and if anyone questioned him, there was nothing to be questioned about his love of dancing and the motorcycle riding, football playing, other side of Buddy. Buddy's star shined bright from early on. It was just undeniable. He sang great, he danced great, played football great. He was a man's man and very Type A.

Patsy Swayze was an inspiration to all. Her life was about quality of dance. I'll only say just great, dear, wonderful things about that woman. Patsy Swayze was amazing.

The other thing is that it really was *Urban Cowboy* with John Travolta that caught fire in that whole period of the first go-around of the popularity of all things Western here. I can tell you that Patsy, back in the mid-sixties, had the attention of people on Broadway and in Hollywood for the quality of her work.

FINAL COMMENT: She's a person I will always keep dear in my heart.

Credit: David Shutts.

Krissy Richmond.

CHAPTER THIRTEEN

KRISSY RICHMOND

Professional Dancer, Choreographer, Broadway Performer, Actress

Interview: March 16, 2019

I really appreciate you taking the time to do an interview.

The Swayzes are very, very special to me. Both Buddy and Patsy were really good to me, and so I would do anything for either one of them. I wish they were both still here. . . .

   The last time I saw the Swayzes, I had Thanksgiving with them in L.A. in 1997, when I was on the road again. Donny was there and he was not married at the time. I don't know his wife, but I'm so glad that he found someone. That is really great.

I saw that you made a few comments in Patsy's obituary.

To Channel 11 [KHOU.com].

If we go back to when you first met Patsy, did you start taking dance from her?

Actually, no. I grew up in Beaumont. My teacher was Marsha Woody and she and Patsy became very good friends. My teacher was more classically oriented. At the time, her studio didn't have a consistent jazz teacher. So Marsha asked Patsy if she would come over a couple of times and teach jazz in Beaumont, and that's how I got to know her. She was basically one of my first jazz teachers. Patsy had the Houston Jazz Ballet. My teacher had a small little civic company, but it was more classically oriented.

We did all of the festivals together. . . . I remember being in New Orleans and seeing Buddy in ballet class, and that was before we made the connection between the two companies. We'd always been sort of separate. As we grew up, I was more classically oriented. I think it was the late sixties, maybe, at Jones Hall. It was way before I finished high school, but Patsy invited my partner and me to come and guest with the Houston Jazz Ballet. So we did *Les Sylphides*. And then they did their jazz, all of the pieces she had choreographed. It was right before Buddy left. I remember that [performance] really, really specifically. I have a review of it. If I can find it, I will make a copy of it and send it to you.

Note from author: *Here is a brief excerpt of the above-mentioned review by Ann Holmes from the* Houston Chronicle *of the* From Bach to Rock *performance of the Houston Jazz Ballet at Jones Hall. "Exploiting the current film idyll, Mrs. Swayze developed the 'I Love Story Pas de Deux'—and why not? Young Patrick Swayze, sturdy and dashing, partnered petite brunette Nikki D'Amico in a stylish rendezvous. . . . High point of the second act comes in the excerpts from 'Les Sylphides' in a version by Marsha Woody of Beaumont featuring Kriss Richmond and Edmund La Fosse of the Woody Academy there. Ms. Richmond was beautiful and admirably secure in her prelude solo . . ."*

So basically, Patsy knew me when I was really young.

How young do you mean?

I would say eleven, twelve. We kept in contact because our teachers were so close. And then we all left. Buddy left first. Before I finished high school, I went to the Washington School of Ballet in Washington, D.C. Everybody went off to do their thing. I remember reconnecting, not directly, but I started dancing professionally. I was with the Houston Ballet and I had a lot of friends in New York. We'd go to New York and we saw Buddy dance with the Eliot Feld Ballet. I know we said hello or whatever. I kept up with Patsy. She knew what I was doing.

The biggest reconnection happened when I was a principal with the Houston Ballet. This was after Patrick did *North and South* and

Dirty Dancing and became a big star. *Dirty Dancing* was 1986, 1987, I think. This was 1991 and the Houston Ballet had been invited to the Dorothy Chandler to perform. I was featured in all of the ballets.

Wow. What an accomplishment!

Right. I called Patsy because they all moved out to L.A. She had a school in Simi Valley. So I called her, and I said, "Patsy, you're not going to believe this, but we're coming to L.A., the Houston Ballet, we're going to be at the Dorothy Chandler." And she said, "Oh, my gosh, we're going to be there and maybe you can come out and teach when you are here." And I said, "I would love that."

I got to my dressing table at the Dorothy Chandler on opening night, and there were two dozen yellow roses on my dressing table from Patsy and Patrick.

Oh, how sweet!

Yes, you know, the yellow roses of Texas.

I remember us finishing a performance and there were all kinds of movie stars there. Shirley MacLaine, I remember the best, because she came running backstage. I was looking for Buddy and Patsy, and all of a sudden, I turned around and there was Buddy, peeking around the corner of the entrance to the back stage. I said, "Buddy, what are you doing?" He said, "I didn't want to take the focus away." I said, "Please come out here." They all came out on stage. And everybody was so incredibly excited to meet them. They were so affirming and so excited that we were there and we had made such a big splash. It was so great.

We all went to that really famous restaurant in L.A. and had an opening night party. Everybody was there. I can remember meeting Betty White, and Jack Klugman, and Shirley of course. We were doing a piece by the Andrew Sisters called *Company B*. Two of the Andrews sisters were there.

It was just an amazing opening night and they were so sweet. Buddy and Lisa were the same as they were while we were growing up, and Patsy was the same. They never changed, as far as I was concerned.

So I did teach that week at her studio and she introduced me to Victoria Lawrence, who was a big agent in L.A. At that time, I wasn't really sure if I was going to go back to the ballet or what I wanted to do. I'd always wanted to sing and dance and act, and so I went and met with her in L.A. and she signed me.

I went back to the ballet for a few months, but I was already auditioning out in L.A. starting that year and I ended up leaving the ballet in 1993. Patsy, especially, was so excited. She said, "I just think you can do a lot of things." She was right.

Then I went on the road. I think Buddy was shooting *Ghost* and *City of Joy*. But he had also done—was it *Red Dawn?*—when he got injured. He was riding a horse and he had an accident.

That was *Letters from a Killer*.

Right after that, I had gone on the road with *Phantom of the Opera* and then gone into New York, but they asked me to come back to do a few months replacement in L.A. It was right around Thanksgiving. And so I checked in with Patsy. I would check in with her every once in a while to see how everything was going. So I told her I was going to be in L.A. at Thanksgiving, and she was like, "Well, do you have any place to go?" I said, "No. Not really." She said, "Then you're coming over here." I said, "Patsy, are you sure?" She said, "Absolutely, I wouldn't have it any other way."

I don't remember what year, sometime in the '90s. I had Thanksgiving with them that year and everybody was there—Donny, Buddy, Bambi, Lisa, and Sean. We had a great, great time. I think I stayed until later on in the evening.

Buddy was like, "Krissy, feel my knee." I said, "What?" He said, "I have three screws in my leg from having the accident on the horse." I said, "Because you had to do it yourself, right? You wouldn't let anybody else do it, right Buddy?" He was like, "Oh, of course." And I said, "That's him." That *was* him. He didn't let anybody do anything [any stunts]. He had to do it all.

Then I ended up going on the road in *Chicago* and back to New York on Broadway. I did a lot of different shows. I always talked to

Patsy, a little bit, here and there.

And then the coolest thing happened was that Buddy was coming in as Billy Flynn.

Note from author: *Billy Flynn was a key character (a hotshot defense attorney for accused murderess Roxie Hart) in the musical* Chicago.

I got to have a photo shoot with him. A couple of us did. We really reconnected. Lisa did not come with him immediately. She came in later. So Buddy was there rehearsing and I was helping him go into the show because I had been dance captain. He was great. We had a lot of fun kind of catching up. It had been a long time since I had spent any quality time with him. And it was great. I remember that time so fondly because that was probably the last time that I got to spend any real quality time with him.

We talked about Patsy and the school, and that she was slowing down and kind of pulling back from teaching quite so much, but the school was still open at that time. I said I wished that she could come here, and he said, "I know, but she's going to see it when we're in L.A." He was there for five weeks.

Then he left and went and did the L.A. company. I'm sure they all went to see him up there. I think I called her right after I knew that she had seen him. And I said, "What did you think?" She said, "Well, I thought he was wonderful, but he could have done this or that better." I was like, "Patsy, you got to be kidding me." She was like, "I know, some things never change."

She loved him so much. I know she was so proud of him. He was a wonderful Billy Flynn, so I know that they had a great time seeing him in L.A. do that role.

I left Broadway to go and do some other things. I was doing a show in Seattle. I did get a hold of Patrick one more time to ask him to host an event for Career Transition for Dancers, which was something that I worked with when I was in New York. It never worked out, but he was more than willing to do it, as always. He almost always said yes, especially for the people who had known him for a long time. And that was Patsy, too. She would have done anything for you.

In fact, one story about Patsy that I remember vividly, is that there is a company that Jeannette Clift George started here in Houston called the A. D. Players. It was a Christian drama group. Jeannette was a big-time actress. She had an Academy Award nomination for *The Hiding Place*. She built this company here in Houston from the ground up, but they didn't have a choreographer or anybody who could stage numbers. So Jeanette called Patsy, because she knew obviously who she was and Patsy choreographed everything. She worked all over Houston. Jeanette called her and said, "Do you think you could come and help me?" She was like, "Absolutely." Jeanette told me, "I'll never forget, the next day, Patsy showed up on my doorstep with a boom box because obviously there was no music. She wasn't going to have access to a pianist or anything."

She did everything that she was asked with a smile on her face. It didn't matter if it was Houston or L.A., the biggest of settings, she never changed. She had an amazing work ethic. Her students did really well. She trained some beautiful dancers.

I do remember talking to her one more time, but it was just a pleasant conversation. I could tell that she was very tired. It was probably a year or year-and-a-half before she passed. She lived her life to her fullest. Everybody who knew her adored her. Any student that you talk to is probably going to tell you the same thing. The Swayzes will always be very special.

Do you have any theories or comments as to why, out of all of the kids, Patrick became the star?

I think that Buddy had something really special. He had a charisma. He was such a good dancer. He was a very masculine dancer. He was a heartthrob from the very beginning. That was just natural. He got that from his dad. Buddy had that thing, and everything he touched turned to gold. He was a ballet dancer. He also did carpentry. He did a lot of stuff on the side to make money in New York. He took a risk by going to L.A. and then he landed *North and South*. He was a heartthrob from the very, very beginning. Even when he was really young, he had that thing. He was a star. You just knew it. That's the best way I can explain it.

I think I get it.

You know, you hear a lot of things about how rigorous dance training is, all the discipline needed, all of the hours put in. You hear various stories, like in that movie *One Last Dance*, that harsh dance teacher. How do you think Patsy figures into all of that? I mean obviously she was strict, but it doesn't sound like she was abusive (not that anybody in connection with this book has said so).

Oh, no. That was not her. All the old-school teachers while we were growing up were disciplinarians. They expected certain things and expected a certain work ethic, but I wouldn't say that was abusive. That was just them knowing what was going to be expected of us in the real world. A dancer's life is hard, and they knew that. It takes talent, but it's also a lot of who you know and timing, and so that played into it definitely.

I wouldn't ever think that anyone would have anything bad to say about her. She was a tough, English woman and she ran her studio as my teacher did, with a lot of discipline, because that was what you did. That was how the foundation happened.

So it sounds like Patsy had a great influence on your life.

She did, and maybe it wasn't as consistent as somebody who was with her every day, as I was obviously not really part of her dance studio. She always wanted everybody to do the best they could. She was just as excited about all of us making it into whatever field we chose to go into. She was great. She was always really an affirming, positive influence.

That's wonderful.

Yeah.

You are still teaching, right?

I am, and actually, I'm still performing. I do projects. I choreograph a lot here in Houston. I teach at a private school. I have done a lot of choreography. I just performed in a play back in January. I just do whatever works with my schedule. If a project comes up that I want to do, I try to make time for it. I need to keep my foot in the door; that's why I just went to New York to see my buddy to get my feet back on the ground a little bit.

Houston is a good theater town. There's a lot going on here. The ballet is still thriving, so that's a really good thing.

I am glad to hear that.

Oh yeah, the ballet, the opera, and the symphony. It's definitely an arts town.

Credit: Photo by Geoff Winningham (1990). Courtesy of Houston Ballet.

Houston Ballet former principal dancer Kristine Richmond as Carabosse in Ben Stevenson's The Sleeping Beauty.

Credit: *Inside Houston*.
Used with permission of Dwight Baxter.

Dwight Baxter.

Credit: Andrea Cody/Dance Houston.
Used with permission of Andrea Cody, Leanna Sparacino, and Dwight Baxter.

Rehearsal for Swing Baby Swing. *Leanna and Dwight are in the second row from front, from left 4th and 5th person.*

CHAPTER FOURTEEN

DWIGHT BAXTER

Choreographer, Director, Producer, Broadway Performer, Professional Dancer

Interview: October 15, 2019

When did you first meet Patsy and under what circumstances?

I met Patsy when I was at the High School for the Performing Arts, back in 1971 or 1972. I was about twelve.

So you started taking dance from Patsy when you were about twelve?

On and off at twelve years old.

What did you learn from Patsy? How did she influence you?

What I learned from Patsy was simple: *Get out there and do it.* When you know the choreography, you know what you're doing, and then you know how to present yourself on stage.

She was a great influence on me. She is the reason I am where I am today.

Patsy was a go-getter. At that time here in Texas, segregation was still strong. The whole thing about Patsy, she was the only one who would allow Blacks to dance. All the other dance schools, they didn't allow that to happen. . . . Racial tensions were still very strong.

That was back in the seventies, right?

Yes, in the seventies.

What do you remember the most about Patsy?

She was a lady who allowed you to do your thing, you know. She allowed African Americans to learn something about the arts, the opportunity to learn the arts. She was located in a place called Houston Music Theater, which is a theater-in-the-round, similar to Westbury Music Theater. There are about five theaters like that in the United States. Chris Wilson was running Houston Music Theater with Patsy Swayze. Patsy Swayze was the choreographer for Chris Wilson's musical theater productions, may have been *Rainbow*, *Oliver*, or anything of that nature. . . . Patsy was the one who did all of the choreography.

How long did you know Patsy?

I knew Patsy until the time she died.

That's amazing.

Myself, Ricky Odums, Kathy Singleton, Bobby Walker who has passed on, Dwayne Phelps who has passed on, and Iverson Polk who has passed on. . . . Rita Jackson, Kathy Singleton, and Ricky Odums were the only ones who survived out of the African Americans. Well, Debbie Allen was there also.

That's who are still living today, let me put it like that. All of us were part of Patsy's group. . . . There was another young man named Kevin who was with us, too. We were the only ones who went to New York to work on Broadway, and that year was 1974. We did an operetta called *Treemonisha*, which was started by the Houston Grand Opera Association under the leadership of David Gottlieb. It was a Gunther Schuller production. When I say that, he was the music director. It all came out of Maine, you know, out of that area. We were like one of the first because Gunther was a very, let's say, a founder of Scott Joplin music. *Treemonisha* was operated by Scott Joplin. So we got our big break at that time, between the ages of seventeen and eighteen.

Wow.

Yeah. We also performed at the Kennedy Center. And that was actually the first time we've ever really seen African Americans do opera. Let's put it like this, at that time, we were shadowed from understanding the world of the performing arts, in certain areas, it may have been opera, but we were living in the South. Not that we didn't want to know, we always wanted to know, but we found out. It was wonderful to see so many African Americans who sang opera: Betty Allen, Kenneth Hicks, and Kathy, she sang at the Mets, contract singer at the Metropolitan Opera House. I think she did *Aida*, [and] some of the great operas of Puccini; just wonderful things.

That is wonderful.

Yes.

If you could speak to Patsy now, what would you say to her?

I would say, "Patsy, we're going to honor you here in Houston, Texas."

Because believe it or not, I was the first, to honor Patsy Swayze here in Houston, Texas, for her leadership and her dedication to the world's theater and performing and visual arts, especially her outreach to the African American community. That was Patsy Swayze. So we honored her at a performance at the Wortham Center here in Houston, one of our great performing centers. It was held at the Cullen Theater, here in Houston.

When was that?

Back in 2016. We did honor Patsy along with Ms. Mary Martha Lappe.

Note from author: *Dance Houston's 14th Annual Celebration of Dance was on November 5, 2016. According to the November 3, 2016 article, "Dance Houston's 14th Celebration of Dance" on the* HotinHoustonNow *website: "Patsy Swayze is a choreographer, dancer, and teacher whose kind heart and Swayze School of Dance helped to build the careers of many successful dancers including Dwight Baxter, Kathy Singleton, Leanna Sparacino, ten-time Tony Award winner Tommy Tune, and her son Patrick Swayze."*

Mary Martha Lappe and Patsy Swayze kind of worked together. Mary Martha was in charge of the dance department where we all performed and went to school, called the High School of the Performing and Visual Arts, which was started by Ms. Ruth Denney, a woman of theater and dance who became the dean of the theater department at the University of Texas.

There was a mission that they wanted to start at the performing arts school here in Houston, Texas, like it was in New York. So Mary Martha Lappe, Ruth Denney, Patsy Swayze, a lot of the leaders in the world of dance, even at the Houston Ballet, came together along with Bill Chaison, Eugene Collins (as a matter of fact, his wife was the prima ballerina for the Houston Ballet) and they all came to show us how it's done. If it wasn't for them bringing the company of the American Ballet Theatre, we would not have known what it was really all about.

At that moment, I saw Keith Lee, an African American, along with Mr. Arthur Mitchell, do classical ballet, Tchaikovsky's *Swan Lake*. That gave us the impetus to learn more about the world of dance. You know George Faison, the choreographer and founder of one of the greatest musicals of the world, *The Wiz*. George brought his dance company down there. That's when we saw Debbie Allen, who is from Houston, an alumna of Patsy's high school. She said, "Now you guys; keep doing it." She was at Howard University at the time. She is a little older than us.

Note from author: *Debbie Allen spoke to newscaster Robin Roberts in a 2009 interview about how Patsy took her into her Houston dance school as a child, and how due to segregation, this was not even allowed at the time.*

Debbie Allen, Patsy Swayze, George Faison, Arthur Mitchell, Keith Lee, all those people were just good influences for us to understand the world of dance. We didn't know. A sixteen-year-old child doesn't really know what he wants to do. I took the liberty to say, "I want to learn this. I want to be a ballet master."

After I finished up with Patsy, I went down to New York and started studying with the Dance Theatre of Harlem.

So how old were you at that point?

I was seventeen. I went to Purchase College State University of New

York, in the New York system.

Believe it or not, at that time, her son, Patrick Swayze was my roommate.

When he was with the Harkness Ballet?

Yeah. Buddy was with the Harkness Ballet. We were roommates.

How did that go for you?

It went great, two Southern boys.

He was cool. Buddy was really cool. He married one of our close high school friends, Miss Lisa Haapaniemi. They became husband and wife. They used to do a lot of pas de deux together. It was just wonderful. We all just stayed close because we were all from Texas and we were all in New York together. You know, New York can be kind of unfriendly.

How long did you stay in New York?

I'm still in New York. I live in Houston, but I'm still in New York. I have a new musical called *The Swinging Savoy*, all about the Harlem Renaissance in the days of Ella Savoy, the Nicholas Brothers, Lena Horne, Cab Calloway. It's a musical that I founded. I'm the founding writer of the musical. Ed Went was my partner, Carla Rose co-writer.

I've been doing Broadway since I left Patsy. My first show was *Treemonisha*. I've done at least three Tony award winning shows. This is my life. I'm like a walking encyclopedia when it comes to the theater and show business, because I learned from the best. Patsy was the one who started me off. If it wasn't for Patsy, I don't think any of us would be who we are because [it was] her generosity and her willingness to allow us to come into her studio to learn more about dance. It helped us to say, we want to be dancers. And to see a person like Sammy Davis Jr., who is my idol, to perform. I idolized him.

It's all because of Patsy. And you know what? Patsy and Chris Wilson, because Chris ran the theater, the theater-in-the-round. At that time, we weren't highly favored as people of color.

The kids and I always got along (those just like my age); we wanted to dance the same. The parents were something different, but that's that situation. But anyway, we got past that. So now we're all just loving dancing, seeing each other to this day, Nancy Schmidt, Zetta Shook, so many. They were all Patsy dancers. There's another young lady, Molly. She's a major dance critic and fine arts critic here in Houston, Texas. She's been doing that for almost thirty years for the *Houston Chronicle*. She is just wonderful. She handles *Zest Magazine*, which is like the Arts and Leisure section of the *NY Times*. . . .

Tour of Dance Theatre of Harlem: 40 Years of Firsts, which was the year that Arthur Mitchell started the company over forty years ago in 1969. I was part of that whole beginning.

Note from author: *This was a traveling exhibition. "The Dance Theatre of Harlem has made history in the 40 years since it was founded in 1969 by Arthur Mitchell and the late Karel Shook.*

Focusing on the discipline of dance, Mitchell brought ballet to Harlem and DTH evolved from a school into a world class company as its artists became powerful ambassadors for all of America.

Highlighting Dance Theatre of Harlem's 40-plus year history, this magnificent exhibition celebrates the history and art of dance with 22 costumes, set pieces, videos, photographs and tour posters from four staged ballets including: A Streetcar Named Desire, Creole Giselle, Dougla, *and* Firebird. *Dispelling the belief that ballet could not be performed by those of African descent."* University Museum at Texas Southern University.

Dwight Baxter was responsible for bringing this exhibit to Houston and to Texas Southern University.

I kind of love the fact that I'm still around to see great things happen, like the years of Dance Street of Harlem, like finding ourselves through the world theater and the performing arts, people of color. I feel wonderful; coming to the time of the Harlem Renaissance, which is now 100 years, a century, which started the Great Migration. I'm still around to produce a musical and write a musical about the Great Migration. My consultant is Mr. Maurice Hines, who as you know lived that era with his brother, Gregory Hines. If it wasn't for Maurice and Gregory, I don't think all of us who came from Houston and Patsy, would have stayed in New York because we never heard of a show closing without them giving you a warning. *Well, I have to pay my rent.* . . . But that's show business and that's how we learn about show business.

And when you see greats like the late Sammy Davis and Liza Minnelli come back stage. We're doing a show on Broadway called *Grind* by Hal Prince. I met my idol and to hear him speak, "This is what show business is all about, man, you got to take it. You got to move on to the next show." Like Shirley MacLaine says, "We're gypsies."

You know, all of it just led to great things from working with Patsy. I worked with Raquel Welch in Las Vegas, Tahoe, Paris, London, and Australia. It's just wonderful.

I met a man named Sterling Clark who was also a Patsy dancer from Houston. Sterling Clark was a dance captain. He's a great, great human being, a dancer from Houston. He's one of Patsy's students, just a wonderful person, but he's older than me. But it's nice to know that you were welcomed that way because you came from Patsy's. They know you are well-trained.

Note from author: *Sterling Clark was born May 1940 and died September 2015.*

It seems like she taught so many people. I mean into the thousands, maybe.

Yeah, right. She taught a lot of people.

At that time, a lot of dance companies, we used to call it the Southwest Regional Ballet Festival, [which was] where I first saw Arthur Mitchell and Mr. David Howard with his company. All of the great masters, even Robert Johnson, would come to Houston or come to Texas and teach at the festivals and hopefully [we could] get a scholarship to go study in New York. If it wasn't for Patsy, we would not have known about all of these other great people.

Wow. That is just so amazing.
Tell me more about being roommates with Buddy.

He was a great person. We were cool together. We were at two different ballet companies studying dance, classical ballet. He was just a good person.

He was who he was when you see him in his movies, like *Ghost*. He went and did *Grease* on Broadway. Buddy was just a good guy. Most people, when you say Buddy, who are you talking about? We called him Buddy. *Dirty Dancing*; that's Buddy, that was him. The thing when he did the *Road House* film; that was Buddy, that was Patrick Swayze. He loved the outdoors. He had a ranch in New Mexico, him and Lisa. He was who he really was.

I miss Patsy to this day, because, you know, she's always been a great influence. . . . I mean she gave us a break. I wouldn't be talking to you today, if it wasn't for knowing what Patsy was all about and why God put her here on this Earth to say, "I'm going to teach you how to dance."

It just sounds like she was so amazing. She touched so many people's lives.

Oh yeah, she was. She didn't get her just due here in Houston. That's why I gave the dedication to her in one of our performances. We had people who had worked with her to receive her flowers. Of course, I got permission from Lisa and Donny to do that.

In 2016?

Yeah. It was at the Wortham Center here in Houston, at the Cullen Theater in the Wortham Center, similar to Lincoln Center in New York, where you had three or four theaters on one ground.

So I sing great praises for Patsy because she gave us our start.

You hear things about how dance teachers, in general, can be. She wasn't like that?

No. No. She had kids. She's a mom. She's a dance teacher. She knew what it was all about. She knew what it would take.

She was a true Luigi and Jack Cole dancer. Those were particular dance styles.

I'm not a dancer, so I'm trying to keep up.

Jack Cole was a certain dance style, like similar to Bob Fosse. She was a great Luigi dancer as well. She came out of that family, that era, kind of the things that you would see on some of the early TV dance shows, like you know maybe the Perry Como show. Those old days, that was Patsy. The old hullabaloos; that was Patsy's style, you know, and then she kind of moved into the trendier things.

She was about technique. You had to have the classical technique in order to do her work. That's very important, classical technique. That's the same with like Arthur Mitchell; you had to have the classical technique in order to compete on the international level, because anywhere in the world, the thing about dance is you just say: *tombé pas de bourrée*, and every dancer from any country in the world, any continent, will know exactly what you're talking about. Dance has its own language. . . .

Mr. Bill Chaison. He was a man who studied with Patsy and worked for the Alvin Ailey American Dance Theater. He was also a big influence on all of us. He was like Patsy's partner in recruiting students to our school. He was just a wonderful person to help us understand the world of dance. Bill Chaison was from Galveston, Texas. . . . He passed a while back.

I'll never forget when he came to class. He came out and started teaching class, and he had on a pair of tights. I must have laughed my butt off. I said I would never wear those. Guess what? I wear tights.

That's hilarious.

Didn't want to take them off because that was the only way to show the graduation of your body, your legs, your feet: learning how to point your feet, learning how to flex your feet. So essential. It's like an athlete, you have to get the muscles and the strength, to do the jumps, to do the pliés. Those were very important. I didn't understand it. I was a kid from the South.

You bring up a good subject, you know, about male dancers.

I thought all male dancers were gay. And so, by me, you know, not being gay, I just said, "Well, okay, I still want to do it" because when I saw Gene Kelly, Fred Astaire, and Sammy Davis, I said, "No, I can do this." Then like Keith Lee from American Ballet Theatre. He was a great guy. He was one of the first African Americans, all classical ballet. It was phenomenal to learn more. When I got to New York, I said, "Oh, it's just a job, learn how to dance. Make the girls look beautiful."

You've had so many wonderful experiences.

Oh yeah. I go from Houston to London.

Wow. What about Paris?

Paris. Germany: Dusseldorf, Frankfurt, Munich. Italy: Palmetto. Israel: Tel Aviv, even Australia: Melbourne. Dance takes you all over the world.

I know this may sound corny, but I think dance can bring people together.

It really can. That's why I'm doing the musical called *The Swinging Savoy*, because the Savoy ballroom was the only room in Harlem in those days of segregation (heightened in the thirties) where Blacks and whites danced together. They didn't care about anything. They just wanted to dance, sing, play music, and that's where they all came, from downtown to uptown. Everybody jumped into the Savoy ball-room, Mogil's place, "The Home of Happy Feet," and just danced to the big band sounds of Duke Ellington, Benny Goodman, you name it, that's what they did. That's what this musical is all about that I'm doing right now.

Is the musical being performed now?

We're going to start our Historical Black College and University Tour, as well as visiting universities like Texas A&M, University of Texas, Notre Dame, Howard University, NYU, and then we are going to try, of course, to make it to Broadway. Mr. Maurice Hines is the narrator of the show. . . .

It's been a century. The ballroom was the only place where they could all dance together. They could go to the Cotton Club, but it was a little different. They would let you in, but you came in through the back door. But they still performed onstage. All of the movie stars wanted to come up to Harlem. It's amazing, the whole era: The Harlem Renaissance, the Great Migration, coming from slavery into a new world. When I say a new world: wow, we have a new place in society, a new citizenship here in the United States of America. That's why you had the Langston Hughes', Zora Neale Hurstons, and all these people, Marcus Garvey, Marquis Dubois, and the great entertainers. All they could do is one thing: practice. They didn't have TVs. They didn't have the internet. That's how they became so great. Even the Scott Joplins of those worlds.

It was just a wonderful time for us. That's why I look at it and compare 2020 to 1920. No young men wore their pants down to their butt. They had more pride in themselves. When I say pride, they just wanted to look like gentlemen. Women wanted to look like women. I mean the fashion was exquisite back then for women. So that's what's so great about that era and that's the whole purpose of having this tour and this production.

Preferably we'll go to Broadway to show, "This is what it's all about, America." Because American music is jazz music, music that we created. It's about the Lindy Hop and the Lindy Hop dancers. And we celebrate the Lindy Hop dancers in the musical.

I want to see it.

This is a musical that we've been working on for a few years. It's just going to get better and better. These kids tap their butt off. They tap dance, you haven't seen tap since back then. We created the Nicholas Brothers' routine of *Stormy Weather* for this particular tour, staged by Mr. Maurice Hines.

That sounds awesome.

It's all about moving forward, thanks to Miss Patsy Swayze. That's why I can just run it off like I'm drinking water, thanks to Patsy Swayze. She taught me this. I'll tell you another person who can run it off like this is Debbie Allen.

How did Patsy accomplish all that? It seems like her students, like you, and so many people, are sort of following in her footsteps.

Well, you know, we're not nine-to-five people.

Right, exactly.

We are people of faith who are going to make it in the world of the theater and the performing arts.

So many people who were her students have branched out and they're doing their own things.

Molly with the *Houston Chronicle*. We're here. Debbie Allen was one of the best success stories to come out of Patsy's, along with her late son, Patrick Swayze. The great thing about it, when we all got to New York, we all came together as one.

Not only that, I had an opportunity to be assistant choreographer with Lester Wilson, Michael Peters, Joe Layton. Those are great choreographers. . . . These are the guys who took care of the great ladies of Vegas: Lola Falana, Ann-Margret, Shirley MacLaine; you know those people, [and] Raquel Welch, Diana Ross, Cher, Mitzi Gaynor, Debbie Reynolds: my great, great, dear friend, the lady of *Singin' in the Rain*. Thanks to those guys' extension, [it] brought us into their extension. Some of them are not still around, but we all worked with them. I worked with Bob Fosse.

I know you are a choreographer.

I do choreography and I do direct. I'm more on the producer or director side because I do not move as fast as I used to. I say, "Listen, watch me do it one time, after that you're not going to see it again."

I teach master classes. Even with the Harlem Renaissance, we do a master class with our renaissance on: the Lindy Hop, the Big Apple, the different dances of that era, even tap, along with Miss Carla Earle.

She is a wonderful person I am working with. They're all in the new *Cotton Club* movie, *Cotton Club Encore*. They did the first and second one with Maurice and Gregory, Carla Earle, all the greats.

It's been wonderful working with Mr. Frances Ford Coppola and Mr. George Faison: he's the man who set it off in 1973, *The Wiz*. Even before then, there was a musical called *Purlie* that Louis Johnson did that brought us into that whole scene. He was like the African American Bob Fosse, Louis Johnson. He was in the New York City Ballet. He was a favorite of Jerome Robbins.

That tribute you had for Patsy, I keep thinking about that. It sounds so beautiful.

Yes. As a matter of fact, Kathy Singleton received the flowers for Patsy at the tribute.

FINAL COMMENTS: I am also a part of everyone's career to be a great dancer and to be a great human being. I remember this book Patsy gave to me before I graduated from high school, *As a Man Thinketh*. She passed it on to me.

Credit: Lynn Lane. Courtesy of Dance Houston. Used with permission of Andrea Cody, Dwight Baxter, Katherine Singleton, Leanna Sparacino, Harrison Guy.

Dance Houston's 14th Annual Celebration of Dance, November 5, 2016, The Wortham Center. Honoring: Mary Martha Lappe, Mitsi Shen, Patsy Swayze. From left to right: Andrea Cody, Dwight Baxter, Mitsi Shen, Mary Martha Lappe, Katherine Singleton, Leanna Sparacino, Harrison Guy.

Used with permission of David Greiss.

From the 1976 TUTS production of Gigi *at Miller Theatre in Houston. Left to right, Donny Swayze is the second performer and David Greiss is the fourth performer.*

CHAPTER FIFTEEN

DAVID GREISS

Former Marketing Director for Theatre Under The Stars, Performer

Interview: March 31, 2019

I saw you quoted in the Channel 11 [KHOU.com] article after Patsy had passed. Did you take dance lessons from Patsy?

I did. I did indeed. The majority of our relationship kind of stemmed through an organization, I'm sure you've heard of, here in Houston, called Theatre Under The Stars [TUTS].

Yes.

Okay, so I was in the first Humphrey School class that they had in 1972, as a teenage actor wannabe. I started doing a lot of shows for TUTS. There was a bunch of us that started. They didn't really have a resident company, but a lot of people were cast in many shows, over and over and over. Frank Young, who was head of TUTS—and was very close to Patsy, as they had done shows together in the past—had encouraged me. I was primarily a singer and an actor, but they kept putting me in the ensemble and then they wanted me in the dancing ensemble. Frank kept saying, "You know, you really need to go take some dance lessons." I said, "I'm not sure where to go, what to do." He said, "Go talk to Patsy. She'll take care of you. She'll mentor you. She'll get you where you need to be."

Note from author: *From a September 17, 2013 article "Patsy Swayze was known for her kindness" written by Molly Glentzer, for the* Houston Chronicle:

"Former arts administrator Jim Bernhard said Theatre Under The Stars founder Frank Young was among her students, and she choreographed the group's first production, Bells Are Ringing, *in 1968."*

In an obituary, it was noted that Frank Young worked on more than 300 productions; including doing composing, conducting, and choreographing.

But of course, most dancers start when they're very, very young. So for me, starting at seventeen, eighteen, nineteen, whatever that was, was a little bit more of a challenge. But she absolutely took me under her wing. I started taking tap classes, and ballet classes, and jazz classes.

I never was as good as her kids, but I certainly got better than when I started.

Well, that's good.

Needless to say, today I am not a theater dancer.

What do you do today?

I will give you a very, very short background. I actually work part-time at a small equity company called Stages, Stages Repertory Theatre here in Houston. They do about twelve shows a year. They do musicals, plays, [and] new works. They have a Latinx Festival. I actually retired from my full-time job and am working part-time at the box office just for something to do.

My journey from when I knew Patsy and doing shows with TUTS—I really wasn't as fabulous as some of my co-performers and realized I was going to struggle economically. I actually got in the travel business for about twenty years. When I sold my business, I went to work for Theatre Under The Stars. I was the director of marketing for twenty years.

Wow!

Then I retired from that position in April of 2016. So that's sort of my background.

There was a story here in the online article about Patrick stopping by after football practice. Do you remember this?

I do, because we were in class. I actually never called him Patrick.

Nobody ever called him Patrick.

Buddy?

Buddy. I actually kind of thought Buddy was his name. I really never even realized his name was Patrick until years later.

So I was in the middle of a jazz class, and it was, you know, afternoon after school, after college classes. I was taking a class at Patsy's studio. Buddy came by with a group of football player friends that he was practicing with. He was actually still in his shoulder pads and his jersey. And he came in and said, "Okay Mom, I'm ready for class." She said, "No, no, no, no. You need to go get ready and your friends need to leave. We need to do this right." I just thought that was kind of cute. He knew he kind of could do anything he wanted; she kind of put him in his place.

So Buddy took classes with you?

He came in and out of classes a lot, you know, at his mom's studio. Really, I actually did more shows with Donny. I did two shows at TUTS with Donny. Actually, I was texting pictures back and forth with Zetta [Alderman]. We just were remembering some of the old shows. You were the reason we were reconnecting and reminiscing. It was fun to go back and talk about this picture I had of Donny and us in tuxedos doing *Gigi*. Just remembering some great old times, that kind of that don't exist anymore. TUTS still exists as an organization, but a very, very different organization than when we were doing shows for them.

What is different about it?

They just celebrated their 50th anniversary. When Frank was alive and head of the organization, he was one of these old-time, grand theatrical producers. When we did *Oklahoma*, he would put a live horse and carriage [onstage]. . . . When we did *Gone with the Wind*, he had the burning of Atlanta, and the carriages exiting the stage over the hill at Miller Theatre. When we did the first *Scrooge*, he wanted Scrooge and Belle to be dancing on an ice rink. When we did *South*

Pacific, he actually built a waterfall for [the song] "Bali Hai" in half of the orchestra pit. It was the days before social media, when producers could do things like that. It was sort of bigger and grander than life.

Now TUTS books a few national tours. They do still self-produce, but not as grand a scale. They are an equity company, which they were not back when Buddy, Zetta, and I were doing shows for them. I think because they're an equity company now, the rules for equity require certain things with auditions and places where you audition and all of those kind of requirements. Their casts are not filled with fifty percent of the same people from show to show to show, like they used to be back when we were doing shows. I think that's sort of a shame for the kids who are coming up now in the ranks because they don't have the same sense of continuity and commitment from an organization.

Not that there was ever a promise that we would be cast. Sometimes we had our own separate auditions from the general auditions. And they went, "Okay, you're in." We did one little combination, and they went, "Okay, you're done."

Now it is a different world. Now they are paying equity wages. They're more specific and more open about the audition and casting process than they used to be.

I think the last time I actually saw Patsy was when I was marketing director at TUTS. We used to have a thing called the American Musical Theatre Award, which Frank had started. One year, Patsy was the recipient. She and Buddy flew in from L.A. It was up at the new Hobby Center for the Performing Arts where TUTS was now performing. I'm going to say that this was 2005, maybe.

Is that the same as the Ruth Denney Award?

No, the Ruth Denney Award became part of the Tommy Tune Awards, which is the high school musical theater competition and awards that TUTS actually started and now has spread all around the country and is a huge, huge deal. The first couple of years when TUTS moved into the Hobby Center, Frank Young had wanted to give an annual American Musical Theatre Award. It was in conjunction with the fundraising gala every year.

Jerry Herman, who wrote *Mame* and *Hello, Dolly* was one of the winners of the American Musical Theatre Award, and Patsy was one of the winners of the American Musical Theatre Award. It was something that was given for not many years. I think that they kind of folded that into the Tommy Tune Awards. And then Ruth Denney had passed away and then they named one of the awards after her. Then subsequently, I think that Patsy got that award as well.

Note from author: *Patsy was the recipient of the Ruth Denney award in 2004.*

What type of teacher was Patsy? What was it like to take dance from her?

I would say, especially for me, I think she was very kind and giving and very patient. Especially, like I said, when I started taking dance class, I was very, very late to the game, and so most people in class were much more limber and much more skilled than I was, every step of the way. She was like, "Come on, David, you can do it." She was very encouraging. She was just like a mother to everybody, just very nurturing, that's about the best way I could put it. You knew if you messed up, try it again. "Keep working on it. Let me show you how to do it right. Let me help that."

You read and see that so many of these dance professionals are so haughty. If you're not up to speed the way they think you should be, you're sort of dismissed and they focus on the stars. She wasn't like that. Especially if you were in that Patsy, Frank, TUTS dance inner circle, and were friends with her kids, then you were kind of golden with her.

Do you have a theory as to why Buddy became the star, as opposed to the rest of the kids?

I actually don't, quite honestly. I think once they all moved and everything went sort of California, I wasn't in that inner sanctum loop. Really, I'm only in the Houston loop, not the California loop.

Is there anything else you want to say about Patsy?

I was so excited to get your message and just know that you're keeping stuff of hers alive.

I'm trying. It's very interesting.

I would just say they don't make them like that anymore. She was a very unique, sweet, nurturing individual. I will always be thankful for her support and her kindness.

I had a chance to meet her once very briefly in Houston when the film of Buddy and Lisa came out, *One Last Dance*. I only talked to her for a couple of minutes. There was a scenario, she and Buddy got on our tour bus and talked to us for about an hour. She just seemed like a cool person. She was very impressive.

She would always make time for people, that's what I felt was the nurturing aspect of her. She was very giving, and I thought—for someone as talented and in the position, the theater and dance hierarchy that she was in—she didn't have to be. But it was just in her nature.

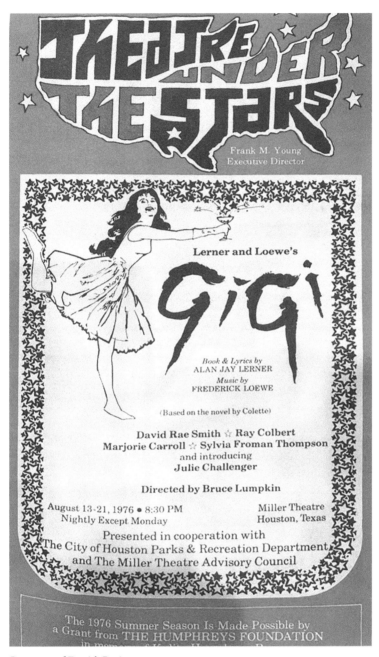

Courtesy of David Greiss.

The program for the 1976 TUTS production of Gigi
at Miller Theatre in Houston.

Credit: Toni Pierce Sands.

Patsy and Rick Odums, 1988 or 1989.

Rick shared that it was a special day as he and his wife, Toni had flown over from France because Patsy wanted to see their newborn son as soon as possible.

Credit: Julie Stewart. Used with permission of Julie Stewart and Rick Odums.

Patrick Swayze, Rick Odums, and Lisa Niemi in Simi Valley in 1986.

CHAPTER SIXTEEN

RICK ODUMS

Founder and Director of Institute De Formation Professionnelle Rick Odums, Ballets Jazz Rick Odums, and Centre International De Danse Jazz Rick Odums, Choreographer, International Professional Dancer

"To Dance is To Live"
By Rick Odums

From the Centre International De Danse Jazz Rick Odums Website. Used with permission of Rick Odums.

"People often ask me why I created this structure: I think quite simply that the answer lies in my own personal history and all of the marvelous things that the art of dance has given me since the first time I entered a school. That day, I not only discovered a world that was completely unknown to me, but I met the person who would be my first mentor and guide, Patsy Swayze. Why mentor? Without a doubt because she did not merely introduce me to dance and its practice, but she lit a passion that I didn't know I had inside of me.

This began with a simple phrase that could be found anywhere in the school, from the classroom to the lobby; the dressing rooms, her posters, brochures, programs for performances, even in the bathrooms: *'To Dance is To Live.'* This simple phrase gave me the desire and the determination to develop this unknown talent that I possessed. Through her teaching and investment, combined with a growing passion for its transmission and creation, and the belief that everyone has the right to a cultural and artistic education—through this activity, this form of communication, we can, as artists, help change and improve the world around us."

CHAPTER SEVENTEEN

STEPHANIE SCHIFF

Chiropractor, Mom, Former Dance Student of Patsy

EMAIL INTERVIEW: November 27 & 29, 2018

When did you meet Patsy and under what circumstances?

The first time I met Patsy was when my mother took me to dance lessons when I was a very small child in the late seventies. Our family moved from Washington State to Simi Valley, CA in 1975. I was five, so it was approximately 1978 when I started dance lessons with Patsy.

What did you learn from Patsy? How did she influence you?

Patsy was amazing. She was an amazing, patient, and precise dance teacher. She taught me and all of her students that as a dance student, you needed to be well-rounded. She insisted on teaching us tap, jazz, and classical ballet at every lesson. Or, we would have jazz and tap on one day, then do ballet on the second day of the week, and then do jazz and tap again on the third day. I just remember going to class several days per week, and having to switch out my dance shoes while at the studio, which made it fun.

Her influence on me was this: She taught me what it was to be disciplined by coming to class each dance day, wearing only pink and black, having my hair up in a bun or ponytail, et cetera. She was the best teacher! I have taken dance lessons off and on since Patsy. I am in my forties now. I have yet to meet a dance teacher who taught the way she did. She taught us students how to move not only our feet, but our toes, precisely in certain positions, the same with our fingers, not just our arms and hands, but every finger had to be in a certain position at certain moments in a dance.

After Patsy, [during] every dance class I would attend, the instructor always came up to comment on my technique, asking me where and with whom I was taught classically. It was always a compliment. I proudly told them all that Patsy Swayze taught me as a child and teenager and it stuck. Even my posture stuck with me. Really! She made us stand a certain way, that "dancer's posture," still have it.

So Patsy taught you what it was to be disciplined. I imagine that carried over to other parts of your life?

Yes, she taught that you need discipline to be good at something, or if something you are passionate about and really want it, you need to really get underneath it, not just practice it on the surface, if that makes any sense.

If you could speak to Patsy now, what would you say to her?

I would say, "Patsy, I really miss having you here to teach dance whenever I feel that passion to dance. I miss the real, classical teacher because there seems to be so few today. You were exceptional, Patsy, and such a kind, patient, and loving soul."

So, they even teach tap online! I took an online class just because I live in a very rural area these last fourteen years (wishing to get back to SoCal) with very few adult dance classes around, and the online tap instructor taught tap dance steps in such a general, non-kosher way. He taught as if the people (sorry, can't call them students) watching did not even know timing (5, 6, 7 and 8). I researched some more online, they are all like this. I know. How can anyone get real dance training online? You can't. You just can't.

Patsy also understood that not only do you need to practice technique, but you also need the brain, the mental practice of routines, which I always had a problem with. I love to dance, but always had severe stage fright, so I could not perform in recitals, or had to be in the back because the routines would just be a jumbled mess in my head. I think it was anxiety, maybe a problem with focus. I went on to become a Doctor of Chiropractic, so it was not a memory/test sort of thing. Whatever it was/is, Patsy understood it. I remember her saying to the entire class, "There is more to dancing than the physical technique part! You have to use your mind! You have to focus!" I remember this so very clearly because I was thinking, "Oh my God, is she talking to me? I had this mental focus problem. Oh, no." Anyway, I look back and realize that half of the students had this problem, not just me, but she tried to help us. She understood me/us.

What contact did you have with any of Patsy's children?

Bambi was in every single class every week, no matter what day it was. It was as if Patsy and Bambi slept in the studio! Must be why Bambi was this angelic, perfect dancer whom every student looked up to, so beautiful.

How old was Bambi when she was always at the dance studio?

I remember Bambi being a young teen, pretty sure she was older than me by a few years.

Patrick would be on the phone with his mom, Patsy, sometimes while she was trying to teach class. I was in awe when he would call. I remember knowing how famous he was after the movie *Red Dawn* came out. By the time *Dirty Dancing* came out, my gosh, just heaven in Patrick! Patrick Swayze's mom Patsy was my dance teacher! It was very "cool." Living in Simi Valley, sometimes he was spotted just walking around town getting groceries. But I was in the studio with his mom, again, for teens and young, twenty-somethings. It was very cool!

So, in conclusion, I have to say with one hundred percent honesty that Patsy was the best dance teacher. I took classes later into my twenties and thirties at very popular studios in Hollywood and downtown Los Angeles, and none of the teachers compared to Patsy. She was one of a kind, *the real deal*. Any successful dancers that are dancing today professionally and were taught by her, they are successful because of her, not because of other existing teachers. It is all Patsy.

Used with permission of Susan Vogelfang.

Susan Vogelfang, production manager, on the set of Liar's Moon.
Patsy was the choreographer. Filmed in Houston, Texas.

CHAPTER EIGHTEEN

SUSAN VOGELFANG

Producer of Movies and Television

Interview: December 19, 2020

I saw your name mentioned in the 2013 article by Molly Glentzer in the *Houston Chronicle* after Patsy had passed.

They called me for her obituary. I was surprised.

So you first met Patsy while working on the movie *Liar's Moon?*

No, I grew up in Houston. So I knew of Patsy. I had met her before. She wouldn't remember me. I did not go to her dance school, but it was well-known in Houston. It was one of the premier dance schools for children. So I grew up in Houston. She grew up in Houston—had her children there. So I knew of her.

When I was the line producer of *Liar's Moon*, Matt Dillon was beginning his career. He had done a small movie called *My Body-guard*. The character was in high school. Anyway, he was cast to be in this movie about Texas in the 1940s and he had a forbidden love. There was a scene in the gymnasium where everybody gets together. It's a big dance. We had a live band. We had cast extras and then we cast Patsy to come with extras and to choreograph the scene in the gym. That's when I first worked with her.

She was known to be able to teach the Texas dances: the shuffle, the two-step, the Texas swing, and the dance called the whip, which was known as West Coast Swing in other parts of the country. Anyway, she could do all the cool dances that you would dance with a partner to a swing band. And so she came and she was great. She knew what to do, she knew how to do it, and she knew how to be on a set and choreograph. The timing of that, probably we shot it in 1979 or 1980; 1981 it came out. So that's how I met her.

Then when I produced commercials, companies would come from New York and Los Angeles to shoot in Texas. They always came to Texas because they wanted something stereotypically Texan. They were looking for ranches or cowboys or cattle or oil rigs, a lot of oil rigs—shot on a lot of oil rigs. Anytime I needed something choreographed, I would call Patsy.

I moved to L.A. in 1981. I was lucky because I had started my career in Houston, worked with all of these companies from out of town, who said, "Look this went really well, if you ever get out there, give us a call." I was so naïve, that's all I moved on. I moved by myself, thinking, "I'll just call them," and it actually worked out. Everybody who I had worked with in Houston hired me at least once. I started a career like the first day I was in L.A.; I was on my way. I was meeting people for the first time. I didn't have a deep Rolodex yet for being in production. I did location scouting. I got to know the companies and the crews. I got to know the city. I eventually moved up to producer again.

When I would have something that required dance, I continued to call Patsy. So she did not [choreograph with me] very frequently, but if I did a movie or if I did a national TV commercial and there was dancing. Patsy could choreograph any style, so I would just call Patsy. She was really easy to work with. She knew how to talk to dancers. She wasn't a screamer. She could explain well. She could teach well. I enjoyed being around her. She was a good 'ole Texas gal. Before I hired her for anything, I had moved. I skipped a step.

The first year I was in L.A., I was all by myself. I had no friends yet. I don't know why, but Patsy heard that I had moved to L.A., found my number, and called and said, "I just want to see how you are doing." "Fine, I just moved here. It's strange." "Come to our house for Thanksgiving." That was so kind. I didn't reach out. I didn't know her that well. So I went out to her home. Her husband had died about a year before. . . .

I didn't meet Patrick. I met her other kids. They were at the Thanksgiving. I was amazed because the Asian daughter she adopted was really quite young, but during that afternoon of feasting around her table, everybody danced. I can't believe the serendipity of adopting a daughter [Bambi] from across the world who turned out to be a fabulous dancer. She was just a girl or maybe a young teenager. She was as if Patsy had given birth to her because she really had the body type, the moves. It was great. It was amazing. It was such a fateful pairing that she would come into that family.

That's about all I remember, just working with Patsy on a few other things. I never knew her very deeply at all. We were more acquaintances who were colleagues. I don't know much about her family other than my personal experience.

She had a good heart. When she invited me for Thanksgiving, I wasn't a very good bet as far as being able to hire her again because at the time, I was scouting locations. I wasn't anywhere near the person who was hiring crews and making decisions. That would be another couple years before that come into mind. So it seemed to be just a really sweet thing to do.

Wow.
When was your last contact with Patsy?

She did a couple of national TV commercials. It might have been for Mountain Dew or some product, hamburger? I would have to go through my accounting book.

That's okay. Was it near the time she passed away in 2013?

Oh, no. I retired in around 2008. I had moved into producing digital effects in the early 2000s. The last big thing I produced was in 2002, an IMAX movie for the state of Texas.

She did *Urban Cowboy* (1980). Of course, that was fantastic. There is *Liar's Moon* (1981).

And Patrick would meet up with Matt Dillon in *The Outsiders*. I don't know what year that was.

It was the first movie for a lot of them. That was 1983.

Patrick was with the ballet in New York. It was a big deal in Houston that one of our own went to the ballet, the dance teacher's son. You're a super fan, so you probably have all of that memorized.

I am a super fan. That is very true. I never thought I would be involved in anything like this. He is the only one I have been a super fan of. I did have a chance to meet Patsy briefly in Houston when the movie *One Last Dance* came out. Patsy did some of the choreography for the movie.

Courtesy of Jessie Mapes.

Jessie Mapes and Debra Winger on the set of Urban Cowboy.

CHAPTER NINETEEN

JESSIE MAPES

Singer, Actress

Interview: March 1, 2020

If we could first do a little back story about you and *Urban Cowboy,* that would be great. How did you get involved and hired for *Urban Cowboy?*

The original story was written by Aaron Latham with *Esquire Magazine.* He wrote it about a group of us who were friends and hung out at Gilley's. The story was about Bud and Sissy, who was my best friend, Betty Jones, and her ex-husband Dew Westbrook. I played myself.

So what happened? They sort of walked into Gilley's, and you were there, and you got hired?

Esquire sent Aaron down to do a story about Gilley's because it was the world's largest nightclub. He started talking to a group at the back [and] found out that there was a love story involving the bull. He just wrote it about Dew and Betty. They had already divorced. They'd been divorced for over a year, but he found a story in it. So that's how that evolved. Then Paramount Pictures, Jim Bridges, got interested in it and decided to do a movie about it.

I had to go read for the part. They wanted me to play myself, but I still had to read for the part. John Travolta was sitting in on the reading. He said, "Oh yeah, no, nobody can do her, but her." I had John's approval. That's how that came about. So Gator [Conley] played himself. I played myself. Norman Tucker played himself.

Everybody else was just brought in from Hollywood to make the story.

So regarding Patsy Swayze, did you have any contact with her?

Yeah, from day one. Patsy came in to meet everybody to see could we dance, 'cause we're all going to be dancing around the dance floor. She wanted to see how we danced, if we could dance. Was there anything that she could instruct us to do differently? She pretty much left the core group of us alone because that was our home, that's what we did every single night.

So are you talking about the two-step?

The two-step, the waltz, the polka, you know, the hoedown. Gator always did a hoedown. Patsy taught John how to do the hoedown.

She also taught him how to do the two-step?

Patsy taught John and Debra the two-step, but John would also go and dance with us. Like I danced with John a lot, just so he could get a feel for dancing the two-step with different partners. Debra would dance with Gator and everybody a lot, and John would dance with me and Betty. You know, whoever he felt like dancing with at the time, he'd go grab somebody to dance. Patsy choreographed most of John's stuff and told him how she wanted it done. He learned a lot, too, just from dancing with the rest of us.

What did you notice about Patsy? What was she like?

She was infectious. She always was smiling. She just had fun. I don't think she met a stranger. I mean, she took me in. So if I was bored and wanted somebody to hang out with, I hung out with Patsy.

I think that was the first movie that she choreographed.

I mean she had a dance studio in Houston, but I didn't know of her before the movie.

I guess after the movie, she ended up moving out to California.

You know, she built a bigger studio and a club, out west of Houston, and opened it up, but then there was a big fire and I don't know how long after the club opened. There was a fire and it destroyed it, and I think after that is when she moved.

I didn't know that.

Patsy and her husband had opened up a club.

I understand from talking to some other folks that some of Patsy's students were in the movie.

Yes.

Did you interact with them?

I did. I couldn't tell you [who]. I think Zetta Raney [Alderman] was one of her students. Other than that, I can't tell you who were students and who were not. When we were on set, we interacted with everybody. When we were off set, there was a group called the Gilley's Regulars and we just all hung out. We were a big family.

Is there anything else you can think of about Patsy in relation to *Urban Cowboy*?

Like I said, Patsy and her husband just, she treated us all like she'd known us forever.

You guys did a 2015 show.

The CMT special. *Urban Cowboy: The Rise and Fall of Gilley's*. Yeah, that was interesting.

Do you have any special memories about filming *Urban Cowboy*?

With Patsy, not so much. With John, yes. With Debra, yes. Patsy was busy, you know, so we didn't hang with her like we did with John and Debra. John and Debra, we'd all grab up and go to lunch together. John would pick us up in the limo and say, "Come on, let's go" and we never knew where we were going. He took me flying on his brand new airplane for my twenty-first birthday.

Wow!

Things like that. Debra and I would go hang out on set when we weren't filming.

There's a lot of great memories. A lot of hurry up and wait. "That was great, but let's try it one more time, take thirty-two," you know, a lot of that. It was awesome and a lot of fun, something that I'll treasure, and something my kids and my grandkids are proud of. It's not too often that your kids can say, "Hey, my mom was in a movie." And you know the fact that I was pregnant through half of it, my oldest son feels like he was in the movie, too.

That is so cute.

Yeah, that was one thing Patsy was worried about was me being on the dance floor pregnant at nine months. But you know, I was still riding the bull at nine months, so dancing was not going to be a big deal.

How old were you when you first started riding the bull?

Sixteen.

That's pretty amazing.

Yeah, but my son was two when I had him on it.

What happened to Gilley's?

Don't know. It caught fire. Don't know why, don't know how. I don't think it was ever determined. It could have been an electrical fire. It could have been any number of things.

How long ago was that?

In the nineties.

This is certainly a lot of cool information.

Everybody loves Patsy. I don't think there was anybody on the set that had anything bad to say about her.

Note from author: *Jessie was listed as Jessie La Rive when she appeared in* Urban Cowboy. *She is currently performing as a singer.*
Gilley's in Pasadena, Texas had the capacity for 6,000 people when Urban Cowboy *was filmed there and at one point was 70,000 square feet. There was*

a falling-out between Mickey Gilley and Sherwood Cryer (the two owners of Gilley's), that ended up in court, and the judge closed Gilley's in late 1989. Then the fire occurred on July 5, 1990 and the cause of the fire was never determined. Currently, there are Gilley's dance halls in Dallas and Las Vegas.

Jessie Mapes and John Travolta who worked together in Urban Cowboy. *Jessie has a fond memory of John taking her on a plane ride for her 21st birthday in his new plane.*

Credit: Jane Carole.

John Travolta and the 5 Singing Sisters. Urban Cowboy.

CHAPTER TWENTY

JANE CAROLE

Friend, Mother: Her daughters were the group 5 Singing Sisters

Tribute: August 18, 2020

We met Patsy when the movie *Urban Cowboy*, starring John Travolta, was being filmed in Pasadena, Texas at Gilley's Nightclub (considered to be the largest nightclub in the world at that time). It was July 1979. Also, at that time, my daughters' 5 Singing Sisters was a country-western singing group with their back-up band, The Circle-S-Band. They performed throughout Texas and the Southwest areas.

Patsy got the girls on the movie set as extras. They had a wonderful time. She arranged for them to perform at two cast parties for John Travolta and the cast.

Later, she invited us to come and visit at her home in California. We did go. However, it was a sad visit for all of us, as her beloved husband had just passed away.

While we were in L.A., the girls "guested in" with a country-western band at a club there, and of course, here comes Patsy with a group of friends.

She was a woman of great inner strength, courage, and determination. She believed in herself and many others! Thank you, Patsy, for caring about us and being our friend.

Courtesy of Tug Wilson.

Still from Liar's Moon. *Tug Wilson is dancing with Vicky Swayze (just right of center, right of Matt Dillon).*

CHAPTER TWENTY-ONE

TUG WILSON

Actor, Singer, Dancer, Pianist, Entrepreneur

Interview: September 16 and 17, 2021

How did you meet Patsy and how long did you know her?

I was in an audition for the movie version of *The Best Little Whorehouse in Texas* in the summer, maybe spring of 1980. I'm watching the auditions. A local choreographer, Glen Hunsucker, was running the audition.

I notice an older girl, 'cause most of the girls were in their twenties. She was in her thirties, and I'm like, that girl can really dance. So they announce the callbacks and I'm called back for the movie and then there are some girls called back, and the girl is not called back. She is sobbing. So I go over to her, and I say, "You were the best dancer out there. Don't be sad. You're just not meant for this project." "You're just saying that because of my mother." "Who is your mother?" And she just starts laughing like I should know who Patsy Swayze is and I don't, at the time. You know, I'm about nineteen or twenty years old. I say, "Well, I can get you a job dancing." She's like, "You can?" I'm like, "Sure."

Note from author: *The girl was Vicky Swayze.*

So I take her with me. I was a dancing cheerleader for the Houston Astros' baseball teams. We had a team of about twelve dancers and I got her a job there. . . . She took to it. We started working together. She would accompany me to all of my gigs that I played piano and sang on. We were pretty much everyday friends for the next two years.

So I involved her with my family. My mother spent a lot of time with her and ran an employment agency and got her some part-time work. We became like the best of friends.

Note from author: *Vicky ultimately was in more than 300 Houston musical theater productions.*

So this was in the spring of 1980, in Houston?

This was in Houston. None of us were really known. We were at the Houston level. Patsy was hired out of Houston to be the choreographer for *Urban Cowboy*, which changed all of our lives because it brought national attention. She was personally choreographing John Travolta. She included us in everything that she did. She had many students and she employed as many as possible, which was the great thing about this woman. She understood that we weren't just doing this to be trained in dance. She could recognize the entrepreneurial spirit and bring it out in the people she trained. It was very important, because our time was coming. A lot of her dancers went to New York and did well on Broadway, but this was going on another level. It was just an incredible time.

So for those two years, I'd say from the spring of 1980 and all the way through the end of '81 (when they went to Hollywood), Patsy was being employed in movies here, in whatever dance scenes there were. And those movies were *Urban Cowboy* and *Liar's Moon*.

I think you said in your Facebook message to me that there were around fifty Patsy dancers in *Urban Cowboy*?

There were fifty Patsy dancers in *Urban Cowboy* and at least fifteen in *Liar's Moon*.

Okay. Wow.

All fifteen people in that movie were friends of mine. They were all those people Vicky and I worked with at the Astrodome. Vicky was my partner in both movies. Once they moved to Hollywood, everything changed.

So what happened to you?

I went to New York immediately. I won some awards that year. I think I was musical theater singer of the year in 1981. I was in college and president of the music department at University of Houston student body. They said there is nothing more we can teach you, just go take a chance. So I got on the plane with six hundred bucks and off to New York I went. I spent many, many years there, about twelve years.

What were you doing there?

Broadway.

Oh, wow!

I played the piano well enough to be paid. So I wound up making more money actually doing that, singing and playing the piano, than from the shows. At the time, they really didn't pay that much. I did many, many shows, many movies in New York.

I wound up at Caesar's Palace in Atlantic City in my own room, playing the piano, and that's when I made the change. You know, I'm in my twenties. I'm making all this money. Why don't I just move to Vegas? Once I did that, live music ended and I never looked back. I went into another career in gaming. I've been doing that for thirty years. I never went back. I just left everything and stopped my career, right then and there. I made a different choice. At that time, I was like thirty-one. I'd never had a real job except singing, dancing, and playing the piano. I didn't know what the other side was. So I purposively stopped my career at the height of it.

Part of it was because of the AIDS crisis. In New York itself, I started the biggest project. I think it still is in the world, for people with AIDS, and produced many, many benefits and things with different stars to raise money at the time to save the union.

What was the name of it?

Broadway Cares. It is something that I created. It still exists today. All the money, at the time, went to people with AIDS, not to research or education. You know, that experience just left me, it went on for years, where no one would help. It pretty much changed my path from what I was doing. I became more involved in the production of things, and I became a producer. And then I changed my life in the early nineties and moved to Vegas.

My relationship with the Swayzes was kind of bittersweet after the eighties. I did go visit Mrs. Swayze. She still kept my picture on her wall and my demo tape playing at all times. The sight of me there was overwhelming for Patsy, for me to be a constant in their lives. So I really didn't have anything more to do with them after the mid-eighties. But the time I did spend, I was in my prime. I was young and she [Patsy] was very instrumental in pushing my career forward.

Patsy came from a very interesting background. Patsy, herself, was a singer with Tommy Dorsey. Patsy was a multi-talented woman and fell in love with the rancher [Jesse]. The father [Jesse] had that rugged appeal that Patrick had. There was something about him that made him very handsome. Unfortunately, he died very young; I think within that first week of them moving to Simi Valley. He walked the dog and had a heart attack.

Patsy made a choice regarding furthering her career, it was '81 or '82. She was given all sorts of movie offers to choreograph and direct. She was hot then. She chose not to do it. She chose to open the dance studio in Simi Valley. Leanna was helping her. They just supported Patrick's career from then on.

FINAL NOTE: I cherish my time spent with Patsy and Vicky.

Courtesy of Michael Pascoe.

Per Michael: "After Patsy opened her studio in Simi Valley, California, she had some of the former cast of West Side Story *take classes that first year. Over the years, we did many shows with Patsy. Here are some of the photos from them." Michael is in the back row, third from left. Bambi is center in next row.*

Courtesy of Michael Pascoe.

Per Michael: "After Patsy opened her studio in Simi Valley, California, she had some of the former cast of West Side Story *take classes that first year. Over the years, we did many shows with Patsy. Here are some of the photos from them." Michael is in the back row, far left. Bambi is third from left in second row.*

CHAPTER TWENTY-TWO

MICHAEL PASCOE

Magician, Dancer, Artist, Writer

Interview: October 11, 2020

I saw you on the SWAYZE Facebook page. I was trying to figure out those photos of Patsy and you answered. I appreciated it so much.

I was with her when she first came to Simi Valley, California. I was one of the first dancers with her.

When was that?

That was 1981. The story that I got from Patsy was that Patsy wanted to retire. She had the Houston Jazz Ballet Company, as you probably know.

Yes.

She came to California and she just wanted to choreograph. She just got off of doing *Urban Cowboy* with John Travolta. She was riding high on that. She thought she was going to get jobs doing that. In the meantime, she wanted to find a dance studio for Bambi. Patsy wasn't happy with any of the teachers in California. She was upset. She was worried about Bambi's training.

She got hired to choreograph and direct *West Side Story* with a theater group called Horizon Players of Simi Valley, California. They had a theater in Moorpark, California, a sister city. They found an old, run-down movie theater and renovated it into a playhouse. My uncle even had it before then; my uncle tried to have rock-n-roll groups there and did not make a go of it. They were doing *West*

Side Story. There was a guy who was supposed to be the director, and he got into a little tiff with them and they fired him. They were using volunteers. They were looking for somebody desperately. They found Patsy, but Patsy didn't want to do it for free. So they did what they rarely did, they paid her. I'm not sure if the other members knew, but I found out later.

So you were in the production?

I was in that production. There was like almost 300 people who auditioned.

Wow!

When it came out that she was going to be the director and choreographer, everybody came out of the woodwork and started auditioning. That was before Patrick, Buddy made it big. Patsy had a name before that. She had dancers that went to Broadway. The first group that she had in Houston, they all left for Broadway, and then she was so happy, because most of these kids were poor and didn't have much, and she was so happy to see their success on Broadway.

So she came to California. She auditioned all of these people. I asked her years later, "Of all the people who auditioned, I know I wasn't really a great dancer, why did you choose me?" She said, "Well, I liked your singing audition."

It was tough. I mean, she worked us hard. What really annoyed her was the fact that nobody knew how to dance. She goes, "I didn't want to do a dance class before I choreographed, but I guess I'm going to have to." So she rented out a place on Los Angeles Avenue in Simi Valley. It was like a mini-mall or something with office spaces. She taught class first to us and then she choreographed the numbers. It was hard work, but we loved it.

You were young, right?

Yeah, I was young. I had just turned twenty-one.

Had you been dancing before that?

The only time I ever danced was in shows. I didn't formally take a class until with Patsy. She had her sons Donny and Buddy, and she had her daughter Bambi, and her daughter-in-law Lisa, and also Donny's girlfriend Denise Eissing.

After that point, she decided to open up her own studio. She used a lot of the students from that production to be her first set of students.

Got it.
How long did you know her?

I knew her from that point, 1981, until her death. I moved to Las Vegas in the early nineties, but I still kept in contact with her. I was her assistant for a long time. I used to travel around with her and help her teach her classes. She had Dan Flores as one of her teachers and also Wayne Pitts. I think she worked with him in Houston, so she talked him into coming to California. And then Karen Mykytiuk, she dated Sean (Patsy's son) for a while. Then, after I was basically working as a full-time magician, I couldn't spend that much time in the studio, so another young woman named Mia Kang took over.

When was the Swayze video? That was after *Dirty Dancing*, right?

That was after *Dirty Dancing*, because they wanted to capitalize on the ballroom dancing stuff. Patsy wanted to do a ballroom video.

This guy Mark Lemkin wanted to do the video. He did this night-club for kids. A lot of the kids in there became famous. They were working stars. I think some of them were on *Kids Incorporated*.

Note from author: Kids Incorporated *was a TV series from 1984–1993. A couple of the kids from* Kids Incorporated *were famous. One of them was Fergie.*

So Mark Lemkin wanted to do this video and I think it was filmed in 1987. I know it came out in 1988. He did it at two locations: Patsy's studio in Simi Valley and the Red Onion, a restaurant and bar in Woodland Hills, CA. (The Red Onion is now closed.) We did the nightclub scenes at The Red Onion. It was kind of like an audition where there were people competing in a contest. They were supposed to come week after week, and they were supposed to be eliminated, and finally at the end they give a prize. It just happened to be the people who were studying with Patsy. A couple of them are real students.

I bought the video years ago.

Did you like it?

Yes, I did. Anything with Buddy in it.

Anything with Buddy in it, yeah. It was so nice that he participated in there. Of course, he worked really hard with us. Of course, I was used to him at that point. I knew him before he was famous. It was no big deal. I told people I knew Patrick Swayze. *"Oh, you do?"* I didn't think twice about it, you know. He was just Buddy to us.

Do you have a theory as to why Buddy became the famous star, out of Patsy's kids?

That's a very good question. I have thought about it.

His oldest sister Vicky, she was the actress, and of course also a very good dancer and choreographer, in her own right.

Donny works all of the time [as an actor].

Why did Patrick make it? I think he had a very good manager [Bob LeMond] in the beginning, the same manager as John Travolta. He laid the groundwork for Buddy. When he died, another gentleman took over. He [Bob LeMond] got him exposed when he got him on *M*A*S*H*, the TV show *The Renegades*, and *Skatetown USA*. He placed him in a really good position. And then of course, they got *Dirty Dancing*. By the way, Patsy did not want Buddy to do *Dirty Dancing*.

So that's true. I had heard that.

She said she thought the name *Dirty Dancing* [meant] it was going to be vulgar.

Another reason why he made it, there was timing of course with the movie. Once the movie came out, I think people saw the sexuality that he portrayed in the movie with the dancing and the machoism. People like macho dancers like Gene Kelly and Fred Astaire.

I've heard Buddy compared to both of them.

Oh yes, especially Gene Kelly. Gene Kelly was very athletic like Patrick. He did a lot of stunts and such. That was another thing; Buddy did all of his own stunts.

Patsy didn't do just dancing, she also taught acrobatics. She also tried to teach me diving, but it was a lost cause.

If you could talk to Patsy now, what would you say to her?

I would thank her for instilling in me the drive and the work ethic and also thank her for not giving up on me. I started when I was twenty-one years old. Even though I was there every single day, it took me a good ten years to really get decent.

So how long did you take dancing from Patsy?

I took from 1981 until I left, '90 or '91.

You went to Las Vegas then?

Yes, I met my wife. She was a dance teacher and we ended up with our own dance studio. Patsy and Buddy were supposed to come to our wedding, but they had other things and they could not attend.

Anybody talk about Big Bud?

A little bit. What would you like to say?

He was a wonderful man. He was always there at the studio when we were there. He always encouraged me. He was a very nice man. He was kind of quiet. He didn't say much. Patsy was more of the domineering person in the relationship. They loved each other so much. There was so much love in that couple. He had a very dry sense of humor. He used to be able to throw jokes at you. He used to come up with these sayings: "You're stranger than a dog," stuff like that, little sayings.

Buddy seemed to do the same thing sometimes.

Buddy really looked up to him. He was devastated when Big Bud died. . . .

She was devastated.

I was close to the family. [Now] I'm hardly in touch with any of the family. I think I briefly talked to Sean at the time Patsy passed away.

What else do you want to say about Patsy?

She struggled to get work as a choreographer, which I think was kind of unfair. Hollywood in the eighties wanted young. Patsy not only had the studio in Simi Valley, but she was also asked by Debbie Reynolds to teach classes at her studio in North Hollywood. Patsy taught classes on Wednesday evenings and Saturday mornings. She got work, but not [as much] as she should have gotten.

Note from author: *Michael gave two examples. He said that Patsy would have liked to have been the choreographer for* A Chorus Line *and* Staying Alive.

That's really a shame.

It was a shame.

What happened with *Staying Alive* was, John Travolta wanted Patsy. He [had] worked with her on *Urban Cowboy* and he thought she would be perfect to choreograph it. He had a place in Santa Barbara. He had this big 'ole tent and he put mirrors in the tent and a dance floor.

Patsy took her assistant, Dan Flores, because he was a choreographer and teacher. They went to the ranch. They worked with John Travolta for like three to four days, to get him ready for the movie. Coincidentally, I was working for Paramount Studios and I happened to go to the ranch, too, when they were there. . . . So she was kind of disappointed in not getting that either.

That's too bad.

She was a good choreographer and was trying to capitalize on *Urban Cowboy*.

She did a couple of other ones. *Hope Floats* [1998]?

She did choreography for Pee-wee Herman's *Big Top* second movie: *Big Top Pee-wee* [1988]. There were a lot of circus acts. She choreographed the jugglers and the acrobats and everybody. She placed the scenes where everybody was supposed to go.

She had a whole list of stuff that she did. She did *Liar's Moon*.

The eighties was also a strange time for musicals. I remember somebody saying that they didn't like the old-style musicals because people just don't all of a sudden sing in the middle of a dance. Of course that is true, but that's not why we go to see a musical.

Note from author: *Patsy also choreographed the movie* Younger and Younger *(1993) and* Letters from a Killer *(1998), which Patrick starred in.*

What else about Patsy?

I remember I was working overtime and I really was sad because Michael Jackson was rehearsing *Thriller* at Debbie Reynolds' studios and one of Patsy's students was in it. Patsy got to meet Michael Jackson and she was so thrilled to meet him. . . .

She was also very proud to be a Southerner.

Also, she said it didn't matter what time of day it was (not that she was a late riser); her first meal always had to be a breakfast, even if it was in the afternoon. She loved breakfast.

She was also a person who was funny. She claimed that she didn't like jokes that much. She used to always make people laugh because she always had something to say to make people laugh. I think that took the tension away when you're dancing and constantly being corrected. It took a lot of the edge off when she would throw in a little bit of humor.

That's good.

She was tough, though. I mean, she was very patient as far as doing the same correction over and over again, but if she found out that you didn't want to work, then all of a sudden, her tone changed. She would be patient and work over and over with you if you made the same mistake, but if you didn't put the work in, then she would get mad.

She was never abusive though, right (not that anyone in connection with this book has said this)?

Never.

Remember, back in those days, she came from the era when some teachers were abusive. They used to throw stuff at people and everything.

Hit people?

I think she had a Russian teacher who I think threw something at her feet. They used to walk by and whack your thigh with a stick while you were doing a pirouette, and that way you would always remember to do your pirouette correctly. She never did any of those things.

Another thing you can't do today that she did, she was very hands-on, which was very important. You have to be able to touch a student to communicate to them what to do with their body.

So you can't do that today because somebody might say it is abuse or inappropriate or whatever?

Yeah, who knows? I haven't taught in a while, so I cannot even imagine what it would be like now.

So you and Patsy taught together for a while?

Yeah. I was teaching with Patsy, and also my wife and I had our own studio.

I have a question. I saw on the *West Side Story* handbill (that you sent me) a dancer named Nikki.

Yes, Nikki Diane, but her real name is Nikki D'Amico. I knew Nikki and I thought she was a very beautiful dancer. . . . Patsy had so many of them. She taught Jaclyn Smith. She taught Debbie Allen and Farrah Fawcett.

Somebody else said Patsy taught Farrah Fawcett, but I have never seen that in writing.

I do remember Patsy telling me one time about [instructing] Farrah.

And then of course, John Travolta.

Patsy said John was very kind and very shy. There was a little girl in the *Urban Cowboy* production who brought him a stuffed animal. One time, he saw the little girl coming by and he put the stuffed animal in his window and he waved to her and pointed, "See? I have your stuffed animal."

John also liked Big Bud a lot.

I have to relay something that Patsy told me (I'm not a witness to). She told me that she set the tempo to "When the Devil Went Down to Georgia." That's the song by Charlie Daniels that was in the movie *Urban Cowboy*. According to the way she told it, she said to Charlie Daniels, "Make it faster." He said, "Well, how fast can you dance?" And she goes, "How fast can you play it?"

I have a photo of Donny because I think he was an extra in *Urban Cowboy*.

He was an extra and he was featured in a certain part where he was dancing with the girl. He was doing a country move, where he had his hand around the girl's neck. I think it was the Texas two-step.

I got to go to Gilley's with Patsy.

Wow.

That was an honor because they treated her like a long-lost daughter.

Gilley's sounded like it was quite a place!

Oh, it was. I think it was about an acre and that was not counting the rodeo that was in back of it. Yeah, you had the main property which was an acre. This bar was humongous. It was just like they show in the movie; they had the punching thing and the bucking bronco and bars everywhere, and in the back they had another acre of property that was a rodeo and sawdust on the floor and everything.

Patsy also had a background in the theater. She used to sing and dance as well. A friend of mine from high school, we did a local production of *Once Upon a Mattress*, and she posted a picture of Patsy. "Oh look, Patsy did the same part as I did."

She was very proud of her family.

Note from author: *Michael sent the program for the Horizon Players* West Side Story *production done in Moorpark, California. This was the first time Michael met Patsy (1981). There is a message from Patsy Swayze in the program:*

Note from the Director/Choreographer

Community theater work can be most difficult, and at the same time the most rewarding for a director. Difficult, because there is never enough time or financial support. Rewarding, as one observes inexperienced, untrained talent develop and continue to grow. Being a recent newcomer to California, Simi Valley, and to Horizon Theatre, I would like to thank the dedicated cast, staff and crew who have given so freely of their time, talent and encouragement.

You have my deep respect and appreciation.

Thank you, Patsy Swayze

Courtesy of Michael Pascoe.

Cover of program for Patsy's West Side Story *production.*

CHAPTER TWENTY-THREE

MIA KANG

Patsy's Dance Teacher and Master Class Demonstrator for Twenty-Five Years

Interview: January 31, 2021

When did you first meet Patsy and under what circumstances?

When I was fourteen (in 1983), I had really wanted professional dance training and I had begged my parents to let me go. They were really hesitant because I spent most of my childhood sick in bed. They were really worried. I started at her studio just very slowly and then I eventually got to go every single day, lots of classes a day. So that became my second home. Eventually, I started teaching for her and I traveled quite a bit as her demonstrator.

You traveled with Patsy a lot?

Yes, she was invited to be a master teacher, because her style of American jazz, to take a class in her style, was really rare and because her style became so popular, she was really in demand. It was mainly as a jazz teacher, but she also taught ballet, tap, ballroom, and country, all over the place.

What do you mean all over the place? Like different states?

Yeah, we went from the East Coast to the South, to Arizona, Las Vegas, just about everywhere. We also went to Norway.

Wow. I had never heard that before.

They are really beautiful, classical dancers, but when it came to American jazz and musical theater, they needed quite a bit of help.

So how long did you know Patsy?

From the time I was fourteen until she died.

Oh, my gosh.
What do you remember the most about Patsy?

She was like a second mother to me. The thing that I remember the most is that her legacy was really how she taught by example. It wasn't just about teaching us steps, it was really about teaching us about respect and how to think as we're in class. So that every time we were doing something, she would always discuss: What is the reason we're doing it? Why is it that we're falling off balance? Why is it that something goes well or doesn't go well?

You know, whenever I went with her to demonstrate her classes, by then she was in her sixties and early seventies, and by the end of the day, when you fly across the country and you're in a different time zone, it's really tough after teaching all day. After teaching all day, she didn't go to her room to rest.

We went to observe other teachers. While she was observing other teachers, she would take notes and we would discuss what went well, how they did things. When we got back to California, I could see different ways that she would talk about things, different ideas that she would incorporate into her own teaching. It was just amazing. Here was this woman who is probably one of the world's top master teachers, continually learning all the time, even from young people who she called kids. She would always say that not everybody can teach and not everybody should teach. She really didn't like what was going around a lot in the dance world at that time, that those who can't dance, teach.

She gave me an appreciation for those teachers who really developed their craft. Unfortunately, after she passed, she was probably the last one. I had grown up studying with all of those great teachers. She would tell me, "Go take this person's class or go take that class." There aren't any teachers like that anymore. There are a lot of beautiful dancers who are also teaching class, but they aren't like Patsy anymore.

What was it about Patsy that was so special that these teachers don't have nowadays?

They don't really have an understanding. They didn't study to be teachers. From the beginning, Patsy always used to talk about how she did study to be a teacher. She studied from her teacher how to be a teacher.

I was also her last teacher that she actually trained. I don't know that she trained anyone else. Her teaching was so phenomenal that many of us went on to become really great teachers. To me, the mark of a good teacher is if your students can turn around and give back what you gave to them.

Are you teaching now?

I did. I only taught until she closed her studio, and now I teach school.

What grade and what do you teach?

I teach science to highly gifted children in middle school. I'm working on my doctorate. It's possible because of what I experienced, in terms of what I was learning with her and when I started teaching for her.

When did the studio close, by the way?

It closed probably three or four years before she died.

Are you still dancing?

No, I was in a car accident.

I'm sorry.

I taught for her for about five or six years after I was in the car accident, but it was really difficult to dance without a lot of pain. When I tried taking dance class at another place, it wasn't the same. I know it couldn't have been the same, but it just didn't feel right.

Did you have any contact with any of Patsy's family?

Yes, I grew up going back and forth. We would go out to Lisa and

Patrick's ranch once in a while. Her family came to the studio. Her daughter Bambi danced at her mom's studio. I knew her oldest daughter Vicky very well. She was like an older sister to me.

Very special.
Do you have a theory as to why Patrick became the star, the famous one, from the kids?

I don't know. He was an incredibly hard worker. He basically had everything: he had looks, he could sing, he could dance, he could act. Everybody loved him. He was incredibly kind and generous to everyone all the time, no matter what was going on. I'm not saying that his brothers weren't because they were all the same way. They came from a family that was kind and humble and multi-talented.

I don't know if you know, but Patsy didn't want to be in show business. She originally wanted to be a doctor.

I didn't know.

Her life dream while she was growing up was to be a doctor. She got hit by a car, and part of her therapy was to start taking dance lessons. There's no doubt that if she had been a doctor, she would have done something also great, like find a cure to cancer or do something else.

She got into the dancing because of the car accident, and maybe because of her kids, she got into the teaching instead of performing?

She did perform quite a bit. I believe there was a show that she left to get married. Then she ended up with her own studio.

If you could talk to her now, what would you say?

I would want her to just really kind of soak in the legacy that she left behind. At the point where I started teaching with her until we closed, we raised a couple generations of kids. The last generation, they're in college now, they're either dancing or teaching. They're still doing wonderful things.

One of the things she always talked about was her kids that she taught in Texas. They all grew up to be actors, and producers, and directors, and choreographers; they did really wonderful things in show business. You couldn't turn on a channel without seeing somebody's show or a kid who studied with Patsy, all the time when I was growing up.

When she came to California, that legacy just didn't stop. It just kept going and going. She had talked a lot of times about getting old and how she should retire. She was used to being so powerful and being able to just get up and go and do whatever she wanted. When she started slowing down, she was kind of disappointed because there were so many things she wanted to do, she couldn't just get them all in. Like she would talk about wanting to produce and direct different shows. As you get older, there are just limitations, and then her eyesight got progressively worse over the years.

I told her that the last generations that she taught are going to be so much more influential, that they are going to influence all of the generations that they come into contact with. I know that she was very humble about all of that, especially in the last month or two before she died. She lost large chunks of her memory between the present and the past, so sometimes she would think something that happened a long time ago happened now. Sometimes she would come back and remember.

She was someone who always wanted to do more or to be better, always wanted to help someone else, those kids, those families who didn't have anything or who needed something, always feeling like there was something more that she needed to be doing.

Wow, I am almost sort of speechless. She is quite a legacy. Are you still in touch with any of the other people from contacts with Patsy?

Just over Facebook. We've drifted apart a little bit.

What else about Patsy?

She could be a difficult person to work with, to work for. She could be difficult in her own way, but I always knew that she loved me. It really made me strong, and that was how I knew that I had creative talent and teaching talent. Otherwise, I would have never known that, you know. And that's really what I want to bring to my own contribution, in terms of my doctoral research and my dissertation: the power of how we teach teachers to teach. It's not about putting them in one class or the other. It's about how we show them to teach. It's not about the twenty books they read or the ten reports they write.

That's a great way to pass on her legacy. Is there anything else that you can think of?

When I was working for her at her studio, we had students who were deaf. We had one with spina bifida. We had quite a few students with ADHD and other kind of issues. I don't know how she taught me to work with them, but she did, that figuring out how twenty or thirty kids come into your class and each one leaves feeling wonderful. They feel invigorated. They leave just feeling better. They leave better than when they walked into the door. If that could be bottled, we could solve so many of our society's problems in terms of how we honor each student. That's why she was such a wonderfully effective teacher. . . .

That's what a true artist is able to do. They're able to take somebody and really help shape them and develop them and mold them into everything they can be. What the world really needs to know is how it is that we teach children. . . .

I think we're all better because we studied with her.

That constant desire to learn is really Patsy. I don't see that in my colleagues in education. I remember that *I have to be a better teacher* attitude that she always had. . . . The mind that was always trying to learn.

That's amazing.

Yes, it is.

I wonder where she got that desire? Was it just something maybe that developed in her?

I don't know. She was multi-talented. This is somebody who could draw and paint and sew and cook. She could do really anything and she did it pretty much better than anybody that you could know. She constantly wanted to know more. Maybe that's why she was good at everything.

Patrick was similar in that way I think. Maybe that's where he got it from, his mom. I don't know that he drew or painted, but all of the sports and all of the challenges in his films.
A lot of people I have spoken to while doing this project say Patsy never really got the recognition she deserved.

No, she didn't, but I don't know if it's possible. Even if she got a little bit, it definitely would never have been enough. I'm not saying it would not been enough for her. The recognition she deserves really reaches way beyond just training dancers or her choreography or her teaching.

Courtesy of Jessie Mapes.

Jessie Mapes at Gilley's from the set of Urban Cowboy.

CHAPTER TWENTY-FOUR

LEON BECK

Country-Western Music Journalist, Editor
and Publisher of *Texas Hot Country Magazine*,
Editor of *Gilley's Country Magazine*

Interview: February 1, 2020

I understand that you interviewed Ms. Patsy Swayze in around 1985 for *Gilley's Country Magazine*. The interview focused on the filming of the 1980 movie *Urban Cowboy*, which she choreographed, and the impact of the movie on Patsy and the United States. When you interviewed Patsy, was that the first time you met her?

Yes. Let me kind of identify who I am in reference to Gilley's and why I did the interview. That would explain me being there. I worked for Gilley's Nightclub in marketing and promotion. My job obviously entailed a lot of marketing and promotion. I was the editor of *Gilley's Country Magazine*, which reported on what was going on with Mickey Gilley, and Johnny Lee, and the entertainers who worked at the club, and the band, and then also a lot of the name entertainers who came out to the club. I would do interviews with them. I would do advance interviews with them. Also, when we had celebrities who came out to the club, I would kind of escort them around the club and get photos. I also did newsletters for Mickey Gilley, Johnny Lee, and the club. I handled media relations, if people came out to the club to do stories, or I would set them up with some other people.

You got the background that Patsy was the choreographer for John Travolta, taught him a lot of the dance steps and the dance moves and everything for the *Urban Cowboy* movie. When she came out to Gilley's, and I think it was like '85 or so, I was real excited about meeting her and doing an interview with her. In fact, I even danced with her on Gilley's dance floor, which was a big thrill for me. What I am going to do now is go over some of the things that we talked about.

Basically, I am going to have to read the article to you and you can pull out quotes you want to use. The article is "PATSY SWAYZE: John Travolta's Dance Instructor in *Urban Cowboy* Now Calls Hollywood Home."

After she came out to Gilley's, she was living in Simi Valley, California. I believe she moved out there after the movie. Then she got into making other movies. She had her own dance studio called Patsy Swayze's Dance Studio and she also directed Debbie Reynolds' Professional Rehearsal Studio in Hollywood. Some of the movies that she worked on at the time that I interviewed her: one was called *Liar's Moon* with Matt Dillon and then she did a movie called *Best of the West*, and she worked on several television commercials, including two with John Travolta for the Japanese market.

I am going to read this [from my article] to you:

"Patsy worked with John at his Santa Barbara home for two weeks before filming started. 'At first he was a little slow at it.' Patsy recalls during a recent visit to Gilley's. 'He's a very methodical person and he wanted to know every detail. He asked a million questions, but once he got the feel of the music, you couldn't stop him. He wanted to practice day and night. In fact, he'd come into my room and get my record late at night and go back and practice.'"

She also talked about what John thought about *Urban Cowboy* and Gilley's.

'I just finished a commercial with him in April, and during a break, while we were re-setting cameras, he said, "Patsy, you know, I've done a lot of movies. I've had a lot of experience, and I think I'm getting better all the time. But the most fun I've ever had in my life was at Gilley's, and I'm dying to do another western movie. I hope we get to do another one soon."'

Now this comment was made in '85, and he has done a lot of movies since then. So as of 1985, talking to Patsy, this was his favorite movie. He did *Saturday Night Fever* and he did *Grease*, and you know, a lot of other movies, too.

After *Urban Cowboy* came out, country music became real popular and dancing became real popular and there were a lot of country-western nightclubs that popped up, a lot of the radio stations switched formats to country music, et cetera.

'*Urban Cowboy* set the whole world country dancing,' Patsy says. 'For months after the film was released, I was traveling all over the United States teaching in universities and at clubs, trying to give them a Texas-style of dance.' "Even though she lives in California, Patsy tries not to lose touch with Texas and Gilley's. 'I've got to come 2,000 miles to hear those Texas accents,' she says. 'I love 'em and I miss 'em.'"

We did stay in touch from time to time after the movie came out.

You said you had a chance to dance with Patsy. What was that like? What do you remember about this experience?

A lot. I love to dance. In fact, I teach dance. I used to teach dance at Gilley's. I was on like a dozen dance shows on the national network called Dance in the USA. I would teach groups of people who came to Gilley's. I love to dance and so I just asked her to dance. We did the two-step. I do not remember what song it was. This was a big deal for me to dance with Patsy Swayze. . . .

I was not on the set when the movie was being made because I was part of the media. I've been covering country music many, many years. It was a closed set to the media. I went out to Gilley's from 1974 on, doing interviews, and then went to work for them in 1982. I interviewed a lot of the country entertainers who came out to Gilley's, including Mickey Gilley and Johnny Lee, who worked there, and Sherwood Cryer, who was Mickey Gilley's partner.

Note from author: *Leon was interviewed for the 2015 CMT (Country Music Television) show* Urban Cowboy: The Rise and Fall of Gilley's.

CHAPTER TWENTY-FIVE

NICOLE POLLARD

Former Dance Student, Dance Coach

Interview: January 16, 2021

When did you first meet Patsy and under what circumstances?

I joined the Swayze Dance Studio in 1985. Gosh, I must have been six or seven. I remember I wanted to take a dance class and I looked through the phone book, and you know, you see the name Swayze, and I thought, oh my gosh, like I had no idea. You know, *Dirty Dancing* was big at the time. It was just a popular name. I didn't really know who Patsy was, but I remember going to a video store and she had released a Swayze dancing video. I think I rented it a couple of times, but I loved [that] she taught all these dances. I was only six or seven, but I watched it over and over and I begged my mom to sign me up there.

I still remember what the studio looks like to this day. Yeah, that's how I met her. I ended up signing up for dance. I started out taking two classes a week, but by the time I was done ten years later, I was there every day. I mean I loved it. I was kind of obsessed.

So how long did you know Patsy?

About ten years when I was at the studio every day. Then I think we just kind of lost touch. I became a high school student, then a college student, and then the studio closed.

I ended up dancing at her funeral. I think anyone who has ever danced under her will tell you she was a force to be reckoned with.

What do you mean by that?

It was this interesting combination of: You respect her. You want so badly to please her and make her happy. You don't mess with her. Her word is final word.

I actually quit dancing briefly when I was probably about ten. My parents went through a divorce. My mom had absolutely no money for dance class, even though Patsy had a reasonable rate. I stopped going. I remember getting a phone call from Patsy, being startled to hear Patsy on the line because it meant I was in trouble because I wasn't there. I remember telling her my mom can't afford it. It was like, "Well, what's your problem? Get your ass to class!" From that point on, she let me dance for free. I don't think I ever adequately thanked her. I don't think in my child brain I knew how to do that as a teenager. As an adult, I look back and go *what a gift*. She let me come every day, unlimited classes, as long as she knew that I took it seriously.

I think she knew that I wasn't going to grow up to be a dancer. I was very good, but I think I didn't have the body type. I think she knew. By letting me come every day for free, she was giving me this safe place to be creative and to learn discipline, to learn all of the things kids that I think maybe nowadays don't learn. I really felt like I had a healthy dose of education. She had that sign on her door that said: "Success is 10 percent talent and 90 percent hard work." That carries over. That's what I remember, and I'm forty years old. I'm not a dancer, but that is the life lesson I picked up from her. I will forever be in her debt.

I am curious now to know how many were dancing on quote unquote "scholarship." I doubt it was only me.

It wasn't only you. I've heard this story many times.

I don't know how she kept that place afloat, but we were all there. Single moms [who had kids who] needed a place to go to be kids and be safe and be creative. I don't think there were any strings attached, that's the crazy part.

I don't think too many people would do that—then or now.

I wish we had adequately thanked her for that.

Maybe she knew how much you appreciated it.

Yeah, I hope so.

So did you have any contact with any of Patsy's family?

No, [except] at the funeral, I danced with Stormie and Charlene. She had a couple of nephews and nieces that were at the funeral that I went to, which was the memorial at the cultural arts center in Simi Valley that Jan Glasband threw. She put it on, or at least hosted it, but a lot of the dancers came back. Her nephews and nieces were there. No, I haven't had any contact with her family except Donny, who I was in a musical with years ago.

Note from author: *An article from the* Simi Valley Acorn *in 2013 quotes Jan Glasband, artistic director for Actors' Repertory Theatre of Simi Valley, "'She helped to shape the concept of what the arts center means to the community and was always supportive of arts programs and dancers," Glasband said. 'Patsy Swayze even received an Educator of the Year Award from the center in 2007 for her efforts to keep the arts alive through her dance studio.'"*

So if you could talk to Patsy now, what would you say to her?

Thank you, for sure, for all the lessons and just giving me a safe place and confidence. A compliment from Patsy was like, you know, it was amazing to get that. I mean she gave them out freely, but you really respected what she had to say.

Also, I have continued her, I don't want to say legacy, but I'm a dance advisor at a high school. It's nothing compared to what Patsy has done in the world of dance. I talk to my kids about her. I tell them what she has taught me. I think I reiterated to them: "Success is 10 percent talent and 90 percent hard work. If your butt's asleep, your brain's asleep." Things I think she said just walking through the studio in her leg warmers. I can still see her now. I think I have tried to pass those things on to the kids that I work with.

That's cool. When you say dance advisor, what do you mean?

I coach a dance team at Golden Valley High School out here in Santa Clarita [California]. I run a dance team. It's mainly lower income kids. It's a Title One school. So we do ask the kids to pay $800.00 at the beginning of the school year to be in the program, because I have to pay for coaching and choreography. On more than one occasion, I've had kids come up to me and say, "I can't afford this. My mom can't afford this." It's just such a funny thing when it happens because I immediately go back to like this is Patsy. This is where I get to pay it forward.

So who pays for it when they can't afford it?

Oh gosh, I fundraise like a nut. I beg, borrow, and steal, which is maybe what she did. I have no idea. You get it from somewhere and it just comes together. You have fundraisers, you have shows, and you make deals with people. You find choreographers who will work for cheap or free or who owe you. I think that's probably what she did. Never do I say, you can't be part of this program—because she never did that.

What else do you remember about Patsy, any other stories?

There is one story somebody told at the funeral. I think it was the studio in Houston that she had and it was not looked at as okay to have Black students. Somebody said something and she just went out, guns a'blazing, and confronted them dead-on. [She said] that she was going to have whoever the hell she wanted at her studio. It was just one of those stories where like you could just envision Patsy doing it. She just had such cojones. She would not stand down.

So do you still dance?

I still do. I tend to hire younger teachers because the kids want younger teachers, but I can still hold my own. I remember Patsy. She must have been in her sixties or seventies when she was at the studio. She could hold her own. She would go out and smoke a couple cigarettes and then come back in and hold her own. She was a dancer, through and through.

Are you in touch with any of the other students?

Oh for sure. I mean, it was a family. Thank God for Facebook. . . . They all have really fond memories, and like I said, nobody really became a dancer that I know of or if they did, it was short-lived. I think it just helped us all to become good people through the arts and theater and dance. Just being an artist, I think, you learn empathy. . . .

She had headshots of everybody she taught, all of her dancers, black-and-white headshots, all around the pink walls of the studio.

So it wasn't necessarily the students who became famous, it was *all* of the students?

All of the students had a headshot. She did have some famous faces on the walls. A lot of them were signed.

Like who?

John Travolta was one. She choreographed one of his movies. She had a giant cut-out of Patrick from his movie *Road House* that she put on the far wall. So when we did turns across the floor, we would spot the giant cardboard cut-out. So when you turn, you spot, and what we spotted was Patrick. She had pictures of Donny and everyone she had met.

It sounds like she probably had thousands of students.

Oh, I'm sure.

What else about Patsy?

She just meant a lot to us. Everyone just wanted to make her happy. You wanted to please her. You wanted to do what she asked of you. You did not want to let her down. I don't know how she really instilled that in us. It was like a healthy fear, but you knew she loved you.

I mean she was never abusive, right (not that anyone connected with this book has said this)?

Oh, God no.

Maybe she was strict?

She was strict, and I think in today's day and age, it wouldn't fly. But I think that's a shame. I think it wasn't strict to the point of berating us. It was demanding more of you because she knew you could do it, and it was like, "Don't give me excuses, just do it." So you really started to expect that from yourself, as well. You know she was creative, so she was passionate. I remember other teachers where pencils would fly across the room. To me, I look at that fondly, as like: *Wow, they really cared enough to be passionate.*

From what I understand, she would teach all styles of dance. Is that what she did at Simi Valley: jazz, tap, and ballet?

Jazz, tap, and ballet. There was no hip-hop. I remember when that came to the forefront, she was not a fan. She was a classically trained dancer. So I think when the times started to change and hip-hop became popular and pop music really became popular, in her mind, she was like, that's not dance. I remember giving her an album called *Color Me Bad*. It was a group back in the nineties. I didn't realize all of the songs were very sexually suggestive, because I was too naïve to know, but man did she give that album back to me, like this is crap. "I refuse to listen to it. I refuse to choreograph to it. You know, throw that in the trash." She was very strong-minded. Tap, jazz, and ballet. Definitely no hip-hop.

I am still thinking about the funeral. How many dancers danced at the funeral?

I want to say a dozen. It was beautiful. Everyone got up and said something. I know they had already had a separate funeral for her. So this was a different group of people, but I think that she had so many different communities that it was just natural to have more than one [funeral].

Did you know Big Buddy?

No, he had already passed. I joined the studio right at the height of *Dirty Dancing*. I think at the first dance recital we had, Patsy gave an outstanding dancer award. I think I still have it. She brought Patrick to give it to the student. He came out on stage. I remember running into him and just being . . . I mean, I wasn't allowed to watch *Dirty Dancing*, but I sure knew who he was, just being gobsmacked. She had chosen a student who was crippled, basically, but still came to dance class [and received] this award, and Patrick presented it to her. It was just a really beautiful thing, but man, you've never seen a bunch of moms rush a stage like that. I don't think he ever came back after that. Yeah, that was the only time I remember him really making an appearance. He didn't really show up at the studio too much, if at all.

He was probably busy.

Yeah. It was her baby.

She sure sucked the marrow out of life. I don't think I realized, I'm only forty-two, but you get tired, you want to sit around. I don't think that was something she did. I don't think that was on the agenda.

I think you're right.
She has a remarkable legacy.

Yeah, she really does. I hope it carries over. I hope people really do remember and pass it on and pay it forward.

ADDITIONAL COMMENT: Everything Patrick was, I think he probably owed to her.

Used with permission of David Krieff.

David Krieff. President and Founder of the Silver Foxes.

CHAPTER TWENTY-SIX

DAVID KRIEFF

President and Founder of Public Relations, Marketing, and Entertainment Companies, President and Founder of Silver Foxes

Interview: August 30, 2021

Photo and text used with permission of David Krieff, President and Founder of the Silver Foxes, from the website silverfoxes.com.

Silver Foxes: Cover of Pilates Video: Back row from left, Tony Tarantino (Quentin), Actress Stefanie Powers, Christine Johnson (Magic), Center left, Sal Pacino (Al), Center right, Nikki Robbins (Tony), Front left, Jenny Crawford (Cindy), Front right, Patsy Swayze (Patrick and Don).

"The Silver Foxes spokespersons are men and women who are parents of some of the world's most recognizable celebrities. . . ."

"The Silver Foxes work to turn around some of the negative stereotypes about aging and the resulting self-perceptions that adversely affect health and well-being. The Silver Foxes are about recognizing the importance of movement and keeping active no matter what level of ability you have. The Silver Foxes Community is also a research team that takes a holistic view in bringing people aged 50 and above the tools to maximize their body, mind and spirit power."

Note from author: *The Silver Foxes also have included: Jacqueline Stallone (Sylvester and Frank), Pauline Fawcett (Farrah), Harry Hoffman (Dustin), Laurie Williams (Robin), and Shirley Simmons (Richard). David Krieff founded the Silver Foxes in the eighties.*

When did you first meet Patsy and how long did you know her for?

I met Patsy, wow this goes way back, probably in 1987 or maybe 1988. I was doing a TV show called *Miami Vice*.

Oh yeah.

Did we meet in Miami or L.A.? I forget where I first met her. I remember the first time that we worked together. She basically took control over everything. Okay. She immediately told everybody how they were doing things wrong, including the instructor. She pretty much did everything. Then she would go in a corner and I would go visit with her. She'd be smoking a cigarette, usually a Marlboro, I believe. I never really saw her without a cigarette in her mouth. She was always smoking a cigarette. You know, I asked her why she smoked cigarettes. She goes, "It's too late for me now to stop," and that kind of thing.

Our relationship was very clear. She is the boss. Even though I'm the boss, I still view her as the boss. *She's* the boss. I lived very well with that. She never said no to me on virtually anything that was within reason. She always joked around with me. We always had fun together. She would do special things for me; like we would do these things that are called "electronic media kits." We would sit down in a studio (this was obviously way before the pandemic or anything), but kind of like what they do now and we would sit and we would do like about ten to twelve hours of interviews in one scene.

She and Sal Pacino were good friends and they were both dancers. They would always get up and dance in the middle of our shows. You know, anything to do with dance, those two were just phenomenal together.

I didn't know that Sal Pacino was a dancer.

Sal owned a dance and music club. It was called Pacino's in Covina, California, for about thirty-five, forty years. Katherin, his widow, could tell you about it. You know, they were great.

Patsy would always, with Dustin Hoffman's dad, Harry, in a nice way, always chide him, joke with him, and tell him he could do better and all that stuff. She would do that with all of the Foxes and everybody that was involved. Cindy Crawford's mom, I think, was in the first one. She loved Pauline Fawcett and her daughter Farrah Fawcett. Pauline is from a place called Champions, Texas. They got along really well. They were like two Southern girls who got together. Basically, Patsy would make poor, little, innocent Pauline do anything that she would never have done before.

It was a very interesting dichotomy between all the Silver Foxes. They had this core base interest in a couple of things: A. Their child is one of the most famous people in the world, and then B. They really all loved to be in good shape, like they really all wanted to be in the best shape they could be, no matter what age they were. Patsy always helped promote that, even with all the joking and all the fun. She would always try to make them do things right and do things easier, ultimately, for themselves and for me. She was just that type of person.

I had many, many talks with her over the years about everything from her sons, her daughters, and her daughters-in-law. She would give me advice. I was going through a divorce, and she gave me some great advice. It really helped me a lot. She became really one of my dearest friends for over thirty-five years. I was twenty-three when

I met her, I believe, so that's when we started our relationship. It continued for that long.

That's amazing.
What did she have to do with *Miami Vice*? I'm going back to that.

Nothing to do with *Miami Vice*. I handled *Miami Vice*. It was an account of mine. I'm from Miami.

I picked up a special promotion for my father (who owned an advertising agency in Florida) called The Villages, like Century Village, a village for retired people. He had hired Richard Simmons to do an endorsement deal where he represented this retirement village. Then we built a ten million dollar, at that point, which was more like a fifty or a hundred million dollar facility, really targeted for seniors. You know, it had swimming pools and trainers and everything from Pilates in there; everything you could imagine, to really get people healthy. A golf course, everything was there. We did probably like a hundred promotions. I had Patsy down [there] and all that. It was phenomenal.

I remember a *Good Morning America* interview where we had ten thousand people in a conga line on the golf course and Patsy was leading it with Sal. Patsy had the perfect conga and so did Sal. And they would lead it, you know, a group of ten thousand. I have pictures of it somewhere. It was pretty amazing stuff.

We did *Oprah Winfrey* and Patsy was great. You could probably get a clip of *Oprah Winfrey* on my website: silverfoxes.com. Then I have a new one coming out called: thenewsilverfoxes.com that also has some stuff on it. Now we have a new group of younger moms and dads and younger celebrities that we're going to be doing this again.

Back to stuff about Patsy. She was crazy about horses. She loved trucks. She loved smoking.

She loved her husband the most. Whenever we talked about her husband, it was clear she would never date another man; she'd never be with another man. Her husband was everything to her and really, when her husband passed away, if it wasn't for her kids and family, she probably wouldn't have cared much about life. I think Silver Foxes came in at a fun time in her life, where she didn't have to put as much energy as she had put into the love of her dear husband. Really, that became clear to me, that nobody could ever replace her husband. She showed me pictures and he was a great-looking guy, and she goes, "Look at this guy. His hair is black. He looks like a stallion horse." She would always brag about her husband, and of course Patrick, and how she taught him to dance, and Donny.

You know, we talked about everything that you would ever talk to a good friend about. Forever, she knew everything about my children, my divorce, and my ex-wife she had met numerous times. You know, just always a dear friend for me.

Every time I did a Silver Foxes project, which there was four of them, she would always be called first or second, behind maybe Jacqueline Stallone, who helped me to create it. Jackie, Sal, and Patsy, those three, you couldn't break those three up. They were really close.

Jacqueline has passed on?

Jacqueline just passed away probably about nine months or a year ago. I wouldn't say *better*, but I was *longer* friends with Jacqueline than anybody. Actually, Jacqueline really was the reason I'm in California. She helped to get me out to California. Yeah, so that was a big deal. It changed my life. I have my family here and stuff. I still live here in beautiful Malibu, California. Jacqueline was very supportive as well.

Talking about Patsy: just one of a kind. She was a real wild one in certain ways. She wouldn't take any guff from anybody, ever. She told her story. She told the way that she wanted things. If she didn't get the way she wanted things, then you were probably going to not be her friend for very long. She was a tough chick until her last breathe, I'm sure she was, and yet the nicest person. She would give her life for her friends, no doubt.

Credit: Frank Whiteley. Used with permission of Frank Whiteley.

Buddy Swayze and Frank Whiteley, longtime friend and bodyguard.

Used with permission of Frank Whiteley.

Buddy Swayze and Frank Whiteley,
longtime friend and bodyguard at a red carpet event.

CHAPTER TWENTY-SEVEN

FRANK WHITELEY

Longtime Friend and Bodyguard of Patrick

Interview: June 2, 2021

Please tell me what Patsy was like and what kind of contacts you had with her?

I drove Buddy out to her house in Simi Valley, you know, quite often when we were together and we had the extra time. We went to her dance studio a couple of times. We met her over there. I remember her being like larger than life, very just in charge of her dance studio. All of the kids who were there fed off of her knowledge and she would teach the kids. "Do this. Do this. Do this. Keep doing it." And she would say, "Perfect. Do it again."

When we went to her house, she always had a snack ready for us.

Any comments you could make about the relationship between Patsy and Buddy?

Buddy and I talked a lot about our relationships with our moms and our relationships with our fathers. Our roles were reversed. My dad was very controlling and demanding and his mom was very controlling and demanding. In the long run, it made Buddy a really good person, because it was instilled in him at an early age that, if you're going to do it, you have to do it right, every single time. In dancing, for example, you know, you have to make the moves and the moves have to be correct and perfect so it all flows and looks really good. At first, there was a lot of, "Mom is making do this" type of thing. And then later in life, he realized her guiding influence actually had helped him in life to complete the task at hand.

So maybe not just in terms of dance, but maybe overall in life, in whatever he was doing.

Yeah.

"I got to read the script." It got to the point where there was a pile of scripts, and you have to read them to see if you like them, to see if you want to do them. It's just another thing to do, but he ended up happy to do it because of the influence his mother had on him: *whatever you do, do it right.*

There is a lot of talk since his death that his mom was overbearing and demanding of him. Well, yes, she wanted him to be great, to reach his potential. So she pushed him all the time to reach that potential. . . . He didn't get beat.

Early on, when I came into the picture in the nineties, it was like, "Yeah, my mom's going to demand me to do this." It's just another thing on his plate to accomplish. So there was apprehension going to see her, but once he got there, he had a good time. He enjoyed seeing his mom.

It was forty minutes from Lake View over to Simi Valley.

What is Lake View?

Lake View Terrace, where he lived.

So you mentioned you came into the picture in the nineties.

Yeah, '91.

So you were his bodyguard and friend from 1991 until he passed. So you knew him for a very long time. His death was tragic. It does seem like his legacy is going on in a positive way. Anything else you can think of about Patsy?

She was a big part of his life. He took care of her. When the dance studio ended up closing because she got too old to be able to manage that, he took care of her in Simi Valley and made sure the house was paid for.

Some of the things that you can't really say, because I protected not only his person, but his reputation.

He was apprehensive seeing his mom. He loved his mom dearly, but she frightened him because she demanded him to be perfect.

No one could be perfect, right?

Not perfect like walk-on-water, but just, If you're going to put the effort into doing it, do it and do it right, don't do it half-ass.

As a man as we get into our forties, we're semi-tired and we don't want to be told what to do. It's just another thing to have to go through. He was apprehensive, but every time that we went, both of us had a good time. I had a good time because he got to see his mom and his mom fed us and shared cool stories. He also felt the same way.

Do you have a comment as to what Patsy's legacy is?

Oh, God. I went with Patrick to New York several times on business trips unrelated to dancing. He would go to the dance studios that he had danced at. You know, just pop in and say hi basically, sometimes dance with the people, show different moves. Those people knew his mom.

We went to Houston to the ballet and popped into the middle of the show. His mom had choreographed that and it was pretty cool. She was a guiding influence on many people's lives in dancing.

I found that out doing this book. I mean, I knew it before, but I know it more now.

I know that as a compromise for Buddy to dancing ballet at a young age, there was a karate dojo at the end of the strip mall where his mom's studio was. So she made a deal to teach some of the students some ballet movements and then this dojo guy would teach karate to Buddy as well. It was kind of a trade-off, and it wouldn't be a young boy being a sissy in Texas at that time. He learned that a lot of the movements were ballet-like movements in karate, so he enjoyed that, and it closed those two worlds for him.

How old do you think he was?

He said he was an early teenager. So I'm assuming ten to thirteen, right around there.

The other thing is, when Buddy's father died, Patsy becomes the only parent, and from what you hear and read, Buddy is the oldest son and he steps up.

Buddy's father was a buffer between Mom and Buddy. It was like, "Let the boy do this. Let the boy play football." Buddy really, really liked his father and had a very good relationship, and he was a cowboy, he was bigger than life. He always wanted to be a cowboy and be ranching. When Patrick became somewhat successful, he was able to buy a ranch in New Mexico and fulfill that dream for his dad. So there was a really close buffer there. He always took care of his mom, from that time forward.

I have a cute story. When I was in Houston for the premiere of *One Last Dance*, **Buddy and Patsy got on the fans' tour bus and talked to us for about an hour. We could ask anything we wanted. It was really cool. Were you in Houston for the premiere?**

I don't remember.

2003 I think. It's been a while.
It was very nice that they would get on our bus and do something like that.

Yeah. You gotta remember that Patrick never forgot, you know, where he came from. I think that has a lot to do with his mom's influence.

We were in Atlanta, Georgia and we were filming *Black Dog* outside of a little tiny town. There was probably a hundred residents who lived in that town. We got cut around 2:30 in the afternoon and there were a couple of people who wanted autographs, so he met with them. The line grew to the point where it started getting dark outside. The residents brought food, dinner, out. This parking lot became a giant picnic. They turned on the headlights. We were there until eleven, eleven thirty at night just talking with people.

That's the type of person he was. He was very inviting to everybody. He wanted to know what people thought and why you thought that way. It wasn't from a judgmental point, it was from, *I want to know about you*. He was genuinely that way.

I don't think that you find that many, I don't know what to call them, celebrities or stars, like that. Not that I ever became a fan of anyone else. I mean I never thought I'd become a fan of anybody like this.
I wonder what it was like for you, being the bodyguard and friend and watching all these things, like what you were just telling me about filming Black Dog.

With Buddy, I enjoyed working for him because, not only did we have the professional relationship, but we also had a personal relationship. We enjoyed talking about adventures and camping, whatever it would be, from a spiritual level to, you know, just two boys kicking it.

One of the things that we talked about a few years before he knew he had cancer was, and this started around seven o'clock at night in his kitchen and we didn't end until about 4:30 in the morning.

Oh, my word.

Oh yeah, our conversations went forever.

His mom was a driving force in everything. So there was an ice skating gig that he had with Disney, and a water skiing gig that he did with Disney down in Florida, [and] all the ballet things. He firmly believed that with all of his training and knowledge that he obtained over his whole career, that all this instilled something in him that he felt that he had a bigger purpose in life than just being a movie star. We talked about: *Well, look at all of the people's lives that you have touched with just the movies that you did*. The influence that *Dirty Dancing* had, the influence that *Road House* had, you know, different movies that you did. You touched people. As you talk to them years later, they tell you, "Oh wow, you got me interested in dancing." Or, "You showed me that a guy can dance and not feel like a geek." He thought that he needed to have a bigger purpose.

We talked a little bit. I don't remember exactly what was said.

"Your mom pushed you in directions that you would never have gone, had it not been for her driving force, so what is it that you're supposed to do?"

Then he passed. I think that he's touched many people's lives. You never know. We talked about that; we just don't know how you influenced somebody's life and made a big difference in it.

He certainly influenced my life.

I have a friend, Joshua Sinclair. He wrote and directed the movie *Jump!* (2008). It was the second-to-last movie that Buddy did. I asked Joshua if he thought Buddy had realized how many lives he had touched and Joshua thought he did. So I was happy to know that.

Yeah, he knew that. He wished he had more time. He wished he had a kid. That was his biggest struggle in all of his life was that he personally felt that he should have been a dad. He learned a lot from his dad. He learned a lot from his mom. He knew what things he wanted to teach and how he wanted to be a father. Our parents teach us things and then we learn from them and then we teach our children similar values, but a different teaching step. He had learned that from his mom. He struggled with that constantly. Different roles would come up and he would shy away from them, like *Fatherhood*. He needed it and it was a good script, but it brought in his demons, as he called them. The things that scare you in life, those are demons. He wanted a kid, and it just didn't work.

Both photos:
Credit: Frank Whiteley.
Used with permission of
Frank Whiteley.

*Buddy Swayze and Frank
Whiteley, longtime friend
and bodyguard.*

Credit: Suzette Van Bylevelt/ZUMAPRESS.com.

March 5, 2002: Los Angeles, CA. Left to right: XR One Co-founder CD PARKS, Patsy Swayze, and Sal Pacino on a Hollywood set where they were talking live on a talk-show (which they did throughout the country) about the energy RX vitamins have given them.

CHAPTER TWENTY-EIGHT

KATHERIN KOVIN-PACINO

Colleague, Author

Interview: October 2, 2020

So did you first meet Patsy at the Silver Foxes?

The first time I met Patsy Swayze was at Silver Foxes with my late husband, Sal Pacino, who is the father of Al Pacino, and this was around 1995. Sal and I were engaged at that time. That's when I met everyone from the Silver Foxes.

Please explain what the Silver Foxes is.

The Silver Foxes was the exercise videos created by exercise guru Richard Simmons, along with the late Jackie Stallone, mother of Sylvester Stallone. She just passed this last September. These videos show seniors how to keep in shape. They consisted basically of my late husband, Sal Pacino. . . . They were the parents of stars: Pauline Fawcett mother of Farrah Fawcett, Patsy Swayze, of course who is the mother of Patrick and Donny, of course, Jackie Stallone, mother of Sylvester and Frankie, and Harry Hoffman, father of Dustin Hoffman, and then Laurie Williams, who was mother of Robin Williams. They kind of alternated; they weren't all necessarily together on the same gigs. Sal and Jackie and Dustin's father were on track with all of them.

The last video that was made was a Pilates video, and the one who led everybody was Stefanie Powers. Now, she wasn't a celebrity parent. They used her as, you know, a star. Of course, on that one, there was Jennifer Crawford-Moluf [mother of Cindy Crawford] and Magic

Johnson's mother, who was Christine Johnson, and of course, there was Sal and then there was Patsy. There may have been one other person on that video, but I forget. That was the last video they did.

When was that?

My husband died in 2005, so that was around 2003 or 2004.

What was it like to work with Patsy on the Silver Foxes?

Patsy was fun and energetic and she always shot from the hip. It was fun to hear her speak so fondly of her children, especially Patrick and Donny, who, as you know, are in the business. Patrick was in the business; unfortunately, he died from cancer. I keep in touch with Donny on Facebook.

How long were you in touch with Patsy?

I lost contact after my husband died of a severe heart attack in 2005.

I am sorry.

Thank you.

What do you remember most about Patsy?

Patsy worked with the movie stars on many big films, including the John Travolta movie and of course with Patrick, her own son [on *One Last Dance*].

I remember most her stories about Patrick and how he went to school on the first day and told her, "Mom, I was the handsomest guy in the class." She goes to her husband, Patrick's father, "He's an actor."

That's very cute.
If you could speak to Patsy now, what would you say to her?

If I could say anything to her, I would say that it was an honor to work with you, Patsy. She would take crippled children and work with their legs and even babies and work with their legs, which was phenomenal, I think.

You always knew what she was thinking. Like I say, she shot from the hip. She was a real Southern gal. She loved her husband until he died. She was a great, great, just a wonderful mother to her children. Of course, she had lost a daughter, too. No parent should have to lose their kids before they die, but unfortunately, that happened.

That's what I really admired about her: that she worked with crippled children and she was so good with stars. She was very, very energetic and enthusiastic about her work, and I loved that. She was very, very self-sufficient, a very strong woman.

Did you ever meet Patrick?

I met Patrick and Donny, very nice gentlemen, nice Southern boys. They were very well brought-up, loved the family. That was very nice. I always liked Patrick (I only met him maybe two times) because he was a very sweet guy, very well-loved in the entertainment business.

Some people that I have interviewed have said they thought Patsy and Patrick had similar personalities.

Yeah, the energy about him and you knew what he was thinking. A very nice guy. He just loved what he was doing in the industry and he was enthusiastic, and I liked that. It's good to see.

I came across a photo of Patsy and your late husband, Mr. Pacino. They're on a television show promoting some vitamins. I am thinking of using the photo in my book.

Oh yeah, they did some kind of vitamin thing. They advertised a couple of different things. That would be an honor to my late husband and me.

Thank you. They are both laughing, and I think Patsy is laughing so hard her eyes are closed.

She was a very happy person. I miss being with them and traveling with them and doing things. The seniors loved them. They kept in shape. She was a good thing.

Yes. Sounds like it.
Do you want to say anything about your career?

I'm a contributing writer and going to be in a book that is debuting next month called *Habit One*. It's about entrepreneurial success by Steven Samblis and Forbes Riley. It is definitely going to be a best-seller, already there's a lot of interest in it.

And then I am going to be writing my own book, in the middle of that, about adoption, as I was adopted at birth. It's going to be about my life having to do with adoption, on both sides. So I'm always trying to encourage other writers and be there for them.

Credit: KC.

Charlene Swayze.

CHAPTER TWENTY-NINE

CHARLENE SWAYZE

Entrepreneur, Philanthropist, Special Needs Advocate, President of Swayze Inc., Swayze Ranch Owner, Cloud Café Owner, Wife of Don Swayze

TRIBUTE

Written: September 16, 2021

Although my time was brief with Patsy, I have the deepest love and respect for her! I first met Patsy while she was recovering in the hospital. It was on Easter Sunday (2013) and my special daughter KC and Donny and I brought Easter baskets full of candy-filled Easter eggs. We walked around with Patsy in her wheelchair and Donny pushing her. We delivered Easter eggs to all of the caregivers and patients. Patsy loved us! KC danced for her and Patsy clapped with glee! My special daughter KC and I visited Patsy several times during her recovery. Each time, she treated us as if we were stars; clapping for us.

During Patsy's last days on Earth, Donny, KC, and I were there at her home in Simi Valley to assist her. During the day, we would be in Patsy's bedroom caring for her. Each day, I would brush her hair and help groom her. With the help of the hospice nurses, we would change her bedding and talk to her. During those days, I let Patsy know that I would take care of Donny. I told Patsy she did not have to worry about him. I let Patsy know that Donny and I loved each other and I would take care of him for her.

During those last few days of Patsy's life, KC saw angels hovering over Patsy's bed. KC is nonverbal, which means she doesn't use words to speak. KC uses sign language. She would point above Patsy's bed to several entities. I could not see them, but KC could. She kept telling me they were angels! One time, I went to the store to buy food for the hospice workers [and] Donny stayed with KC and Patsy. Donny explained to me that all was so quiet and Patsy was resting peacefully and KC, who was laying on Patsy's bed, abruptly sat up. KC got loud and was using her vocal cords, making noises of glee, pointing to angels over Patsy's bed! KC kept trying to tell Donny in sign language that there were angels. Donny figured it out. The hospice worker who was there confirmed that special people do not have the veil that is in between this world and the next. The hospice worker explained that "special" people often see angels! It was so comforting to know that Big Buddy, Vicky, and Patrick were there watching over Patsy and welcoming her into heaven! KC and I were so blessed to have been able to honor Patsy in her last days. She was beautiful. We helped to make her comfortable and were able to see that her family was waiting to welcome her into heaven.

The next time we were visited by angels, and now including Patsy, was during Patsy's celebration of life ceremony. I was honored to dance for Patsy on stage. Right before we started our dance, KC got very vocal again, walking down the theater aisle. KC cannot usually walk by herself. I assist her. Yet she was able to walk down the theater aisle with the theater full of Patsy's family and friends. KC was very vocal, trying to tell the full theater that Patsy was there. She was making loud sounds and "angel" arm movements, walking by herself down the aisle. KC wanted everyone to know that Patsy was an angel now and that she was there with us in the theater. It was so spiritual and wonder-filled! The theater was speechless! Gasping! Amazed! And then we did our dance for Patsy!

From the start, KC and I and Patsy had a spiritual connection. To this day we still have it. We are honored and full of respect and love for Patsy Swayze!

Credit: Michael Montfort/Michael Ochs Archives/Getty Images.

Patsy Swayze poses for a portrait holding a headshot of her son in circa 1988.

PATSY AND PATRICK

WHAT PATRICK SAID ABOUT PATSY

In an interview with Greg Hernandez from *Orange Coast* magazine in July 2005:

> For so many years, she has choreographed and nurtured young talent, Swayze says. She seems to give people that belief in themselves against all odds to move on with their life.

During an interview with Alex Simon, "PATRICK SWAYZE: PEACEFUL WARRIOR" in *Venice Magazine* in June 2004, Patrick spoke about the strong, diverse, positive influence of his mother and father on him that began early in his life and always stayed with him. To understand the influence of Patsy on Patrick, first here is what he said about his father Jesse:

> Well, his dad was one of the foremen of the King Ranch, which was the biggest ranch in the world, at one point. So my dad was raised on a ranch. At one point, he was the state champion calf roper. Needless to say, he got me into that stuff from the time I was little. My dad was a really organic, kind of earthy man. . . .
>
> He really taught me so many things that in your younger years are kind of cliche, but as you get older, you realize their importance: like integrity, passion, in your work ethic. I now live my life by most of the things my dad taught me. I think my favorite saying of his would be: "All I got is my integrity. To this day, I ain't never seen a hearse pulling a U-Haul."

Then in the same interview, Patrick talked about his mother Patsy:

That's the other side of me: the intensity, the passion, the drive, the belief in communicating something through the arts. It's all these qualities of my mother's that have really led me down all these tangential paths in my life. My parents were an amazing couple.

A comment made by Patrick about his early start in the arts to Gavin Esler on the BBC *HARDtalk Extra* in 2006:

I was literally born under the stage, grew up with kings and queens and giants and fairies and goblins being my babysitters. Sleeping in theater seats from the time I was little 'cause my mother is a choreographer, so she's choreographed just about every musical ever written.

Patrick and Patsy spoke to each other on the television show *Superstars and Their Moms—Patrick Swayze* (Warner Brothers) in 1989. Here are some of the highlights of what Patrick said to Patsy. Patrick told Patsy that he loved growing up being in the theater. He said that it was remarkable that Patsy had the courage to have the first dance company with Black dancers in the South and how prejudice was not something he and his siblings were raised with by either of his parents. Patrick also told Patsy how much he appreciated what she gave to him, regardless of whether her love was intense or whether he thought that she handled him the right way all of the time. He talked about how both his parents had given him and his siblings so many different opportunities, stood behind them always, and taught them to believe in themselves.

Patrick spoke to Barbara Walters, in the famous post-*Dirty Dancing*, May 11, 1988, ABC *Barbara Walters Special Interview* about him learning from his mother "the meaning of discipline" in a positive way. He stated that you have to work for things and be deserving of it.

Used with permission of Charlene Swayze.

Patrick as a child at the dance barre.

WHAT PATSY SAID ABOUT PATRICK

During the question and answer session I attended with Patrick and Patsy and other fans in Houston at the *One Last Dance* premiere in 2003, Patsy was asked by a fan, "What was Patrick like as a child?"

Very confident. Always wanted to do everything. Always said he could do it (even if he couldn't do it) and would just go do it.

During the 1989 conversation between Patsy and Patrick on the *Superstars and Their Moms—Patrick Swayze* television show, Patsy talked about how her goal with her children had been for them to be able to handle themselves. To reach that goal, she commented that good manners and respect for others and love of neighbors and families helps a person to be centered. She also said that she knew the talent that Patrick had inside and she had to bring that out.

Back in 1991, Patrick was named the "Sexiest Person Alive" by *PEOPLE* magazine. Patsy was quoted in *PEOPLE* as saying that Patrick did not think he should be considered an idol—that he just thought of himself as a regular Texas kid.

Here are some excerpts from an interview with the *Daily Mail* in August 2011. Patsy spoke about Patrick's childhood, his talent, and his illness and subsequent death:

Remembering her son's childhood, she says fondly: 'He was a great kid. Very, very, very energetic, high maintenance, into everything, played every sport, could sing, play the piano, play the guitar, he was just really outgoing, great personality. Lots of fun to be around and very respectful and well-mannered.'

'Patrick started dancing at age three and because I was teaching I would always take him with me to the dance studio and he just loved it. . . . I remember I took him with me when I went to work and I had a maid there to help take care of him. I taught classical ballet, American jazz, tap, musical theatre, a bit of everything but it didn't matter what kind of music was playing he danced.'

'He just automatically had this talent, and the energy and the drive. He was an outstanding athlete in high school. He played football, he played every sport there was. He was a wrestler, boxer, runner. I just remember him being an outstanding athlete.'

Regarding Patrick working while being ill with pancreatic cancer, she said:

However, she was amazed by her son's resilience and determination to keep working. He just kept working right up until the day he couldn't work anymore and never complained.

Speaking about what the future holds for her, Patsy added: 'I spent a lot of years in film and television and stage plays and I had a wonderful life and I'm really grateful for all of it but you know you're not supposed to outlive your children.'

CLOSING

Feisty and demanding, Swayze devoted herself to nurturing talent and potential. "I love watching people develop strong bodies and a sense of self-worth," Swayze told the *Los Angeles Times* in 1991. "To see the child blossom, that's the thrill of teaching."

Patsy Swayze is the perfect example of how one good person following their dreams, passion, and values can influence so many people, and the world for that matter, in such a compelling and positive way. She not only shaped many artists' lives in the fine techniques of performing, but also taught life lessons to those who pursued a career in the performing arts and those who did not. Her value system was instilled in thousands of people who are currently passing it on to the next generations. And if that is not enough, the importance of the performing arts to humankind has also been highlighted and carried forward by the lifelong work of Patsy Swayze.

ACKNOWLEDGMENTS

It is with the utmost gratitude that I thank the many, many people who provided support, love, and expertise to me in the writing of this book.

First of all, I thank with deep gratitude my family, especially my mom, Phyllis Friedman, and my dad, David Tabashnik—both of whom are always with me in spirit and who always encouraged me to be an avid reader throughout my childhood and supported my ventures as an author. I hope I have made you proud. A very special shout-out goes to my brother, Bruce Tabashnik, who helped with the mechanics, details, and character of the book, and for his unwavering support of the book. David Tabashnik, my late brother, is always in my heart, and I will never forget his support of me as an author. I also thank my nephew, Gabe Tabashnik; my sister-in-law, Andrea Mathias; and my aunts, Nedra Kapetansky and Mary Lou Zieve, who are always great cheerleaders for me. A very special shout-out goes to my dear friend, Mary Kiriazis.

I thank with gratitude Charlene Swayze who has provided information, photos, feedback, time, and a multitude of encouragement throughout the entire process of writing this book. She has also written a very touching tribute to Patsy. Probably without Charlene's involvement, I would not have written this book.

I know Bob Howell and Lee Santiwan are with me in spirit, and yes, a fourth book. I thank my friend, Jackie Horner; you are greatly missed.

I thank my dear friend, Margaret for her friendship and all her work as president of the Official Patrick Swayze International Fan Club that made the 2003 Houston experience so wonderful and created so many great memories.

I thank my dear friend, Joshua Sinclair.

I thank my dear friend, Don Frazier.

I thank Dr. O, Dr. Yashinsky, Laurie Saunders, and John Gifford for all they have done to keep me on the path.

I thank my extraordinary book designer, Patricia Bacall, and my fantastic editors, Pamela Cangioli and Kimberley Jace.

I thank my expert attorney, Larry Jordan, who never tired of my endless questions.

I deeply acknowledge the generosity and graciousness of the interviewees for the sharing of memories, information, photos, and time: Jaclyn Smith, Renee Broussard Jongebloed, Patricia Cope Mackenzie, Susie Ewing, Blake McIver Ewing, Pamela Mistrot Rost, Nikki D'Amico, Cookie Joe, Francie Mendenhall, Deidre Russell, Nancy Schmidt, Leanna Sparacino, Danny Ward, Krissy Richmond, Dwight Baxter, David Greiss, Rick Odums, Stephanie Schiff, Susan Vogelfang, Jessie Mapes, Jane Carole, Tug Wilson, Michael Pascoe, Mia Kang, Leon Beck, Nicole Pollard, David Krieff, Frank Whiteley, and Katherin Kovin-Pacino.

I send a big thank-you to Martha McClintock at Getty Images and Florence Combes at ZUMA Press.

I send a big thank-you to Rena Jacobs for her assistance with the Jaclyn Smith photos and interview.

I send a big thank-you to the following people and media for permission for use of their material: *Houston Chronicle*, Charles Bush, Barry Dean, Bill Logan, Bill Ewing, Glenda Alexander, Julie Stewart, Andrea Cody/Dance Houston, David Shutts, Lynn Chung/Houston Ballet, Geoff Winningham, Bonita Cutliff/University Museum at Texas Southern University, Molly Glentzer, Katherine Singleton, Toni Pierce Sands, *Simi Valley Acorn*, Joshua Sinclair, *Orange Coast*, Alex Simon, BBC, and *Daily Mail*. Special thanks to Barbara Geary and Robert Levitt. Special thanks to Gary Hines for assistance with the photo work.

PERMISSIONS

I gratefully thank these sources for giving permission to use their material.

CHAPTER ONE

"She was one of those extraordinary young people": © Jaclyn Smith International. Used with permission of Jaclyn Smith. From the Official Jaclyn Smith Website. All rights reserved.

CHAPTER FOURTEEN

"Patsy Swayze is a choreographer": © 2016–2021. Used with permission of *HotInHoustonNow* website. "Dance Houston's 14th Celebration of Dance." November 3, 2016.

"The Dance Theatre of Harlem has made history": © 2013–2021. Used with permission of University Museum at Texas Southern University from website. January 2013.

CHAPTER FIFTEEN

"Former arts administrator Jim": © 2013 by *Houston Chronicle*. Used with permission of Molly Glentzer. "Patsy Swayze was known for her kindness." Molly Glentzer. September 17, 2013.

CHAPTER SIXTEEN

"People often ask me why": © 2016. Used with permission of Rick Odums. From the Centre International De Danse Jazz Rick Odums website. "To Dance is To Live." Rick Odums.

CHAPTER TWENTY-FOUR

"Patsy worked with John": © 1985. Used with permission of Leon Beck.

"PATSY SWAYZE: John Travolta's Dance Instructor in *Urban Cowboy* Now Calls Hollywood Home." Leon Beck. *Gilley's Country Magazine.*

CHAPTER TWENTY-FIVE

"**Note from author**: *An article from the* Simi": © 2013 by *Simi Valley Acorn.* "Former students, arts community remember Patsy Swayze's passion." Gabrielle Moreira. October 4, 2013.

CHAPTER TWENTY-SIX

"The Silver Foxes spokespersons": © Used with permission of David Krieff. From website silverfoxes.com.

CHAPTER THIRTY

"For so many years": © 2004 by *Orange Coast* magazine. "Power of One." Greg Hernandez. July 2004 (Volume 30, Number 7).

"Well, his dad was": © 2004 by *Venice Magazine.* "PATRICK SWAYZE: PEACEFUL WARRIOR." Alex Simon. June 2004. Re-published June 10, 2015 in "Great Conversations: Patrick Swayze." Alex Simon. Co-editor. The Hollywood Interview.

"That's the other side of me": © 2004 by *Venice Magazine.* Alex Simon. Ibid.

"I was literally born under the stage": © 2006 by BBC. *HARDtalk Extra.* Gavin Esler. 2006.

"Remembering her son's childhood": © 2011 by *Daily Mail.* "I can't watch his films, it hurts too much." *Daily Mail* reporter. August 18, 2011.

"However, she was amazed": © 2011 by *Daily Mail. Daily Mail* reporter. Ibid.

Credit: Murray Goldenberg.

ABOUT THE AUTHOR

Sue Tabashnik published her latest book *PATRICK SWAYZE The Dreamer* in September 2017. This book presents how Swayze's focus on dreams for himself and others sustained him and guided him to live a zest-filled and hopeful life even while dealing with great adversity. Her earlier two unique *Dirty Dancing* tribute books are *The Fans' Love Story: How the Movie* DIRTY DANCING *Captured the Hearts of Millions!* (July 2010) and *The Fans' Love Story ENCORE: How the Movie* DIRTY DANCING *Captured the Hearts of Millions!* (December 2013).

She became a fan of Patrick Swayze in 1988. She was an active member of the Official Patrick Swayze International Fan Club from 2000–2010, which included writing numerous articles for the club magazine. She had the good fortune to meet Patrick Swayze several times at movie screenings and benefit events from 2002–2004, which led her to become an even bigger fan. Sue has worked as a master's level social worker since 1977. Sue has lived most of her life in the Detroit area.

Author website: https://www.likedirtydancing.com

In memory of Patsy Swayze, a donation has been made to the Swayze Foundation by the author.

CPSIA information can be obtained
at www.ICGtesting.com
Printed in the USA
JSHW031702240822
29637JS00010B/44